$60-

TR
90
a43
1995

a.p.

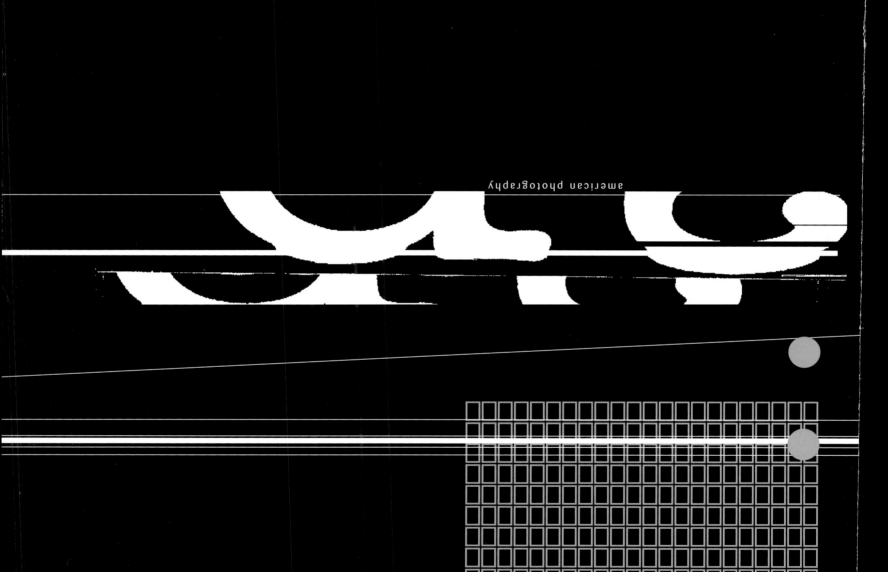

american photography

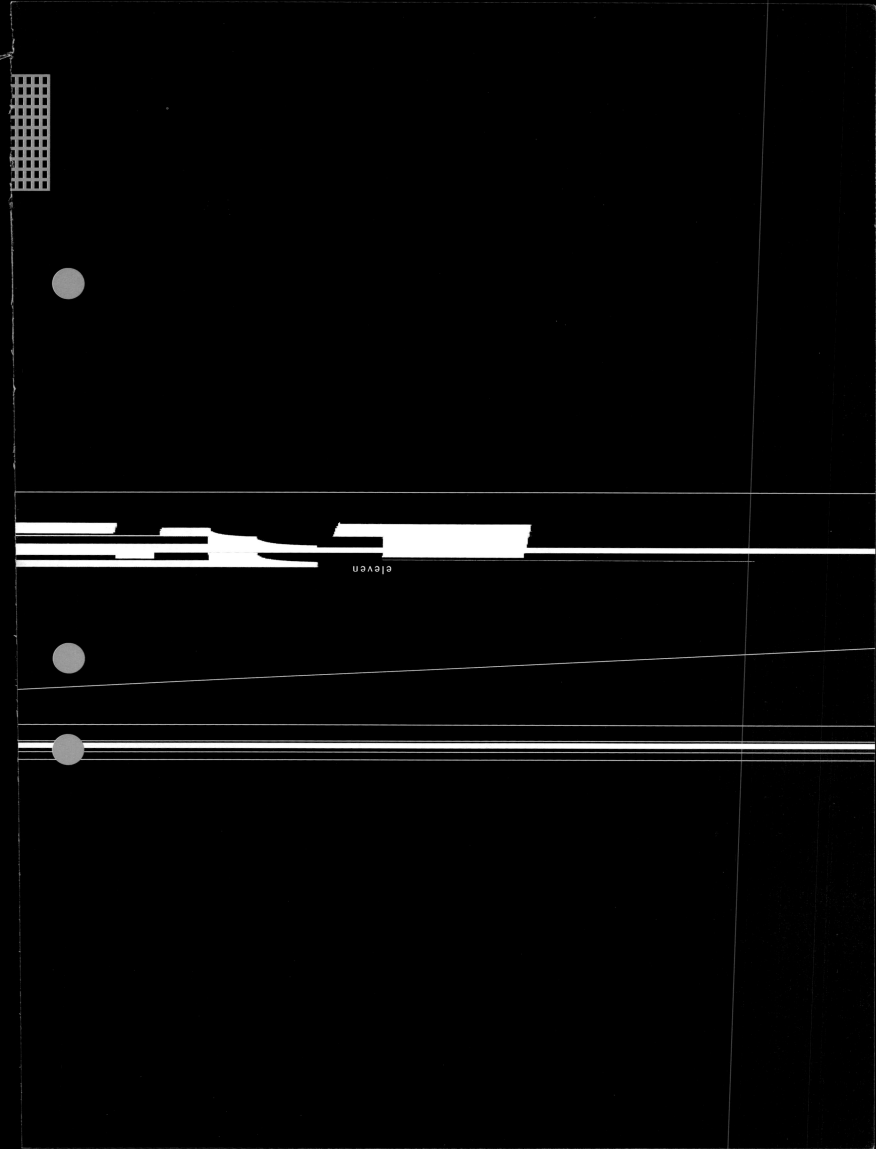

eleven

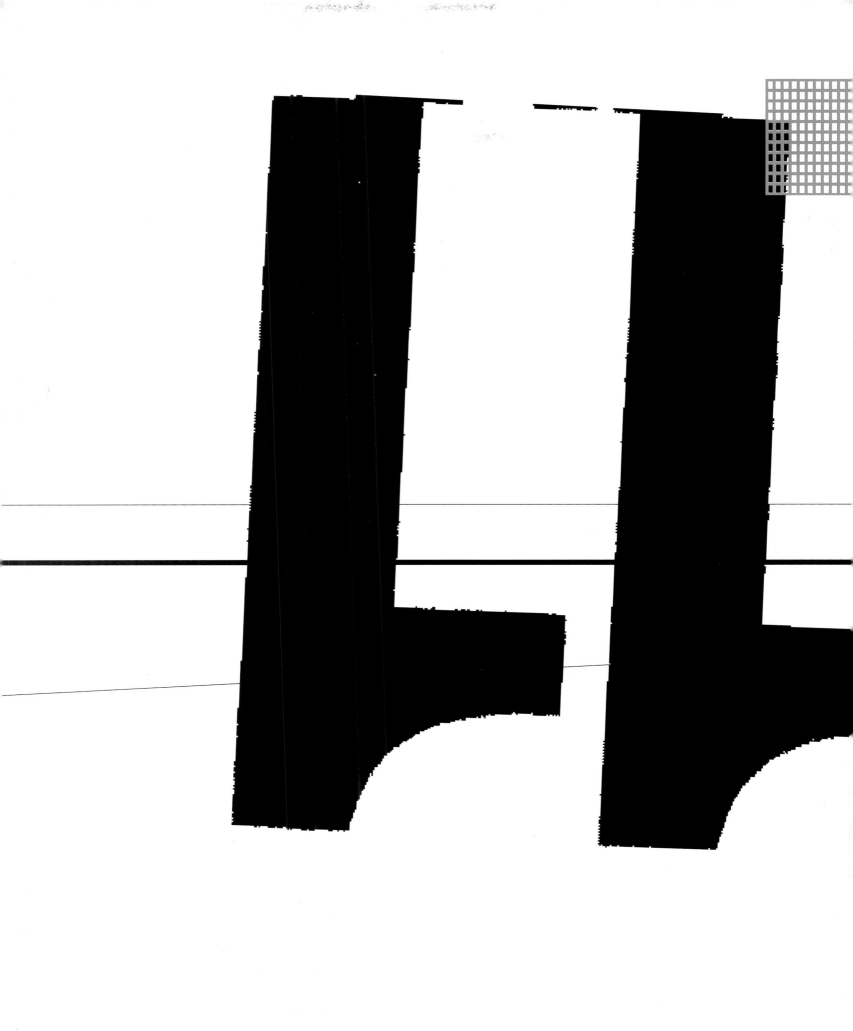

chairman: robert priest
designers: markus kiersztan and petra langhammer
design assistant: heather huprich
production consultant: ilsa enomoto
front jacket photograph: dan winters
back jacket photograph: mary ellen mark
publisher: kenneth fadner
project director: mark heflin
jacket copy and chairman interview: peggy roalf
special thanks to parsons school of design
for providing the space and equipment for the
american photography 11 judging.

captions and artwork in this book have been
supplied by the entrants. while every effort has
been made to ensure accuracy, american
photography does not under any circumstances
accept any responsibility for errors or omissions.
the photographs in this book were originally
published in consumer, trade and technical
magazines, periodicals, newspapers and their
supplements. others were created for
advertisements, promotional design, annual
reports, books, cd covers, catalogs, direct mail,
self-promotion, or were personal works.
if you are a practicing photographer or student
and would like to submit work to the next annual
competition write or call to:
american photography
16 west 19th street · 9th floor
new york, ny 10011 · u.s.a.
telephone (212) 647-0874 · fax (212) 691-6609
distributor to the united states and canada:
d.a.p./distributed art publishers
636 broadway · 12th floor · new york, ny 10012
telephone (212) 473-5119 · fax (212) 673-2887
isbn 1-886212-02-3
distributor to the united kingdom and france:
booth-clibborn editions
12 percy street · london w1p 9fb
isbn 1-873968-84-1
book trade to the rest of the world:
hearst books international
1350 avenue of the americas · new york, ny 10019
additional copies and back issues available through:
american photography
16 west 19th street · 9th floor · new york, ny 10011
printer: dai nippon, hong kong
copyright c1995 amilus, inc.

the jurors

laura harrigan

laura harrigan is the art director of special projects at martha stewart living magazine, where her responsibilities include designing martha stewart's books, premiums, advertising, and collateral material. prior to this, she was the senior associate art director at gq magazine, where she worked with creative director robert priest. before going to gq, laura was the associate art director on the start-up of martha stewart living, a magazine which has won consecutive national magazine awards for photography and design, along with numerous awards from the society of publication designers. before entering the editorial field, laura art directed the catalogs for the now defunct conran's habitat domestic stores. she studied graphic design in new york city and virginia, and lives in manhattan with her husband and son.

kent hunter

kent hunter is executive creative director and a principal of frankfurt balkind partners, a communications agency specializing in design, advertising, annual reports, corporate identity and multi-media/video presentations. under his creative direction, frankfurt balkind's work has been recognized for excellence in design by every major award organization and is included in the permanent collection of the smithsonian. a native texan, kent came to new york by way of nashville, and is a past vice-president of the new york chapter of the american institute of graphic arts. he has judged numerous design shows and given lectures around the country. he is learning to master the point-and-shoot camera.

john c. jay

john c. jay currently serves as international creative director for wieden & kennedy, where he oversees nike's nyc and la campaigns, as well as all work for asia and latin america. recent projects include nike's hoop hop tour, a half-hour television program which aired in japan; microsoft's first brand image print campaign; and the launch design of "ok" soda for coca cola.
prior to joining wieden & kennedy, jay served as the creative director and later as executive vice president of marketing and creative services for bloomingdales in new york city. while in new york, he also was creative director for john jay design, a creative consultancy responsible for international projects including: restaurant interiors; the launch advertising for takashimaya on 5th ave; two books on design (quintessence and elegant solutions for crown publishing); the graphics for the launch of the tokyo dome; and consultation on special projects for dentsu.
jay has received over 150 awards in print and television advertising, package and graphic design, film documentaries and interior/architectural design. in 1985, jay was named as one of the country's most influential people in photography by american photographer magazine. i.d. in 1994 named jay as one of their "top forty" designers in america.

neil kraft

neil kraft has been an award winning creative director for the past 15 years. after graduating from the rhode island school of design in film and photography neil held various jobs in the film production and advertising community. in 1982 neil joined barneys new york where for 8 years as creative director of the in house agency that he set up, he created many award winning campaigns.
in 1990 he joined esprit de corp as worldwide image director. their he created the "what would you do" campaign that redirected esprit's image into the nineties. in 1992 he joined calvin klein as senior vice president of advertising and creative services. there he helped catapult the company in a major new direction. in campaigns with marky mark and kate moss he redefined what calvin klein was all about. in campaigns for obsession and ck one he changed the face of perfume advertising. in addition he radically changed the media mix to bring a fresh approach to fashion's use of outdoor. in 1995 neil formed his own consulting company to help other company's redefine there image. he is currently working with elizabeth arden on world wide image and marketing.

jane palecek

jane palecek has been the art director of *hippocrates*, now *health*, magazine since 1987. previously she served as art director of *the washington times* newspaper and *raintree children's books*.
In addition to health magazine, she still designs children's books and works with students–two activities she finds very comforting.
jane grew up in marshfield, wisconsin and currently lives in san francisco.

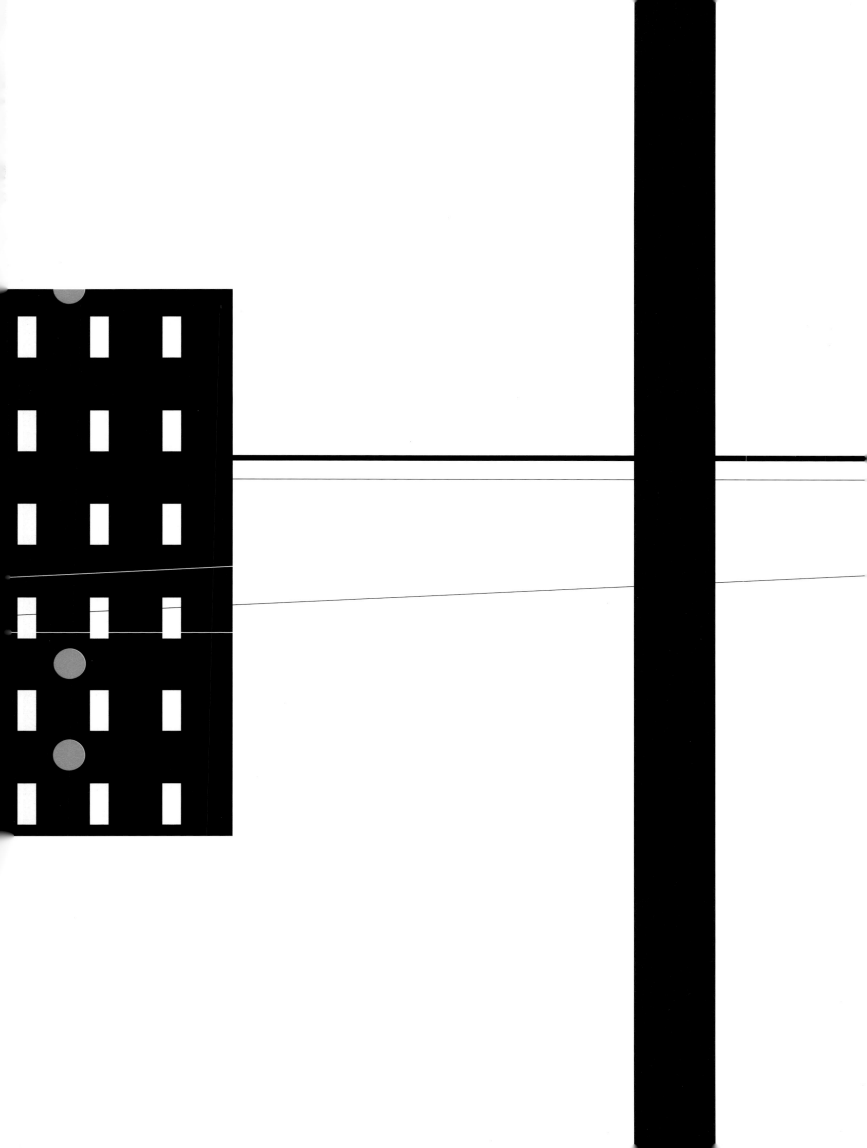

It's an exciting time
for photography right now,

with editors taking risks

by publishing strong,

edgy pictures, and photographers

approaching their

assignments with fascinating

ideas–rather than merely

producing the outstanding

or the beautiful image.

In magazine photography

there's often a danger of

being manipulated by a

subject to enhance the persona–and this year, we are seeing a welcome change away from the obvious

kinds of photos we've grown

tired of. Here are stimulating

photographs with a clear

point of view, with a

wary sense of humor that

hasn't been seen

for some time, with an air of

mystery about them–

pictures that really show photographers at their best.

This book makes room for

the incredibly beautiful

photograph that has no

agenda and also offers a more

serious view of life with

powerful documentary series

by Sebastiao Salgado and

Dan Winters.

Yet even in images of sad

circumstances there

are spontaneous caught

moments that celebrate life with a tremendous feeling of hope.

Robert Priest, Chairman

1 dan winters designer: fred woodward · associate designer: fredrik sundwall · photo editor: denise sfraga · editor: holly george-warren
book title: cobain · publishing company: little brown & co. · memorial celebration for kurt cobain just after his suicide.

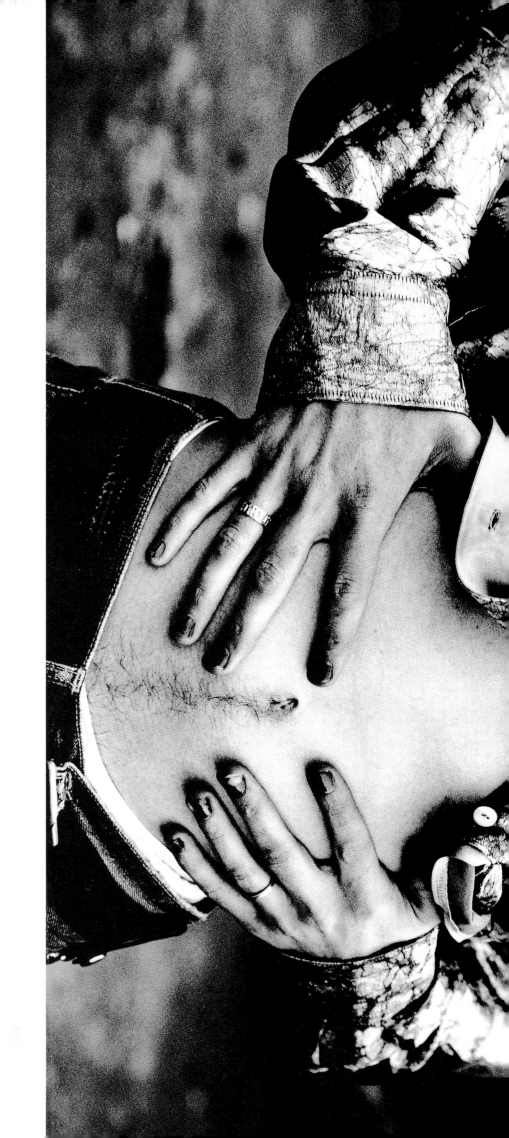

2 anton corbijn art director: markus kiersztan
photography director: greg pond · publication: details
publishing company: condé nast publications, inc.
writer: gavin edwards · kurt cobain for the article *heaven
can wait, november 1993.*

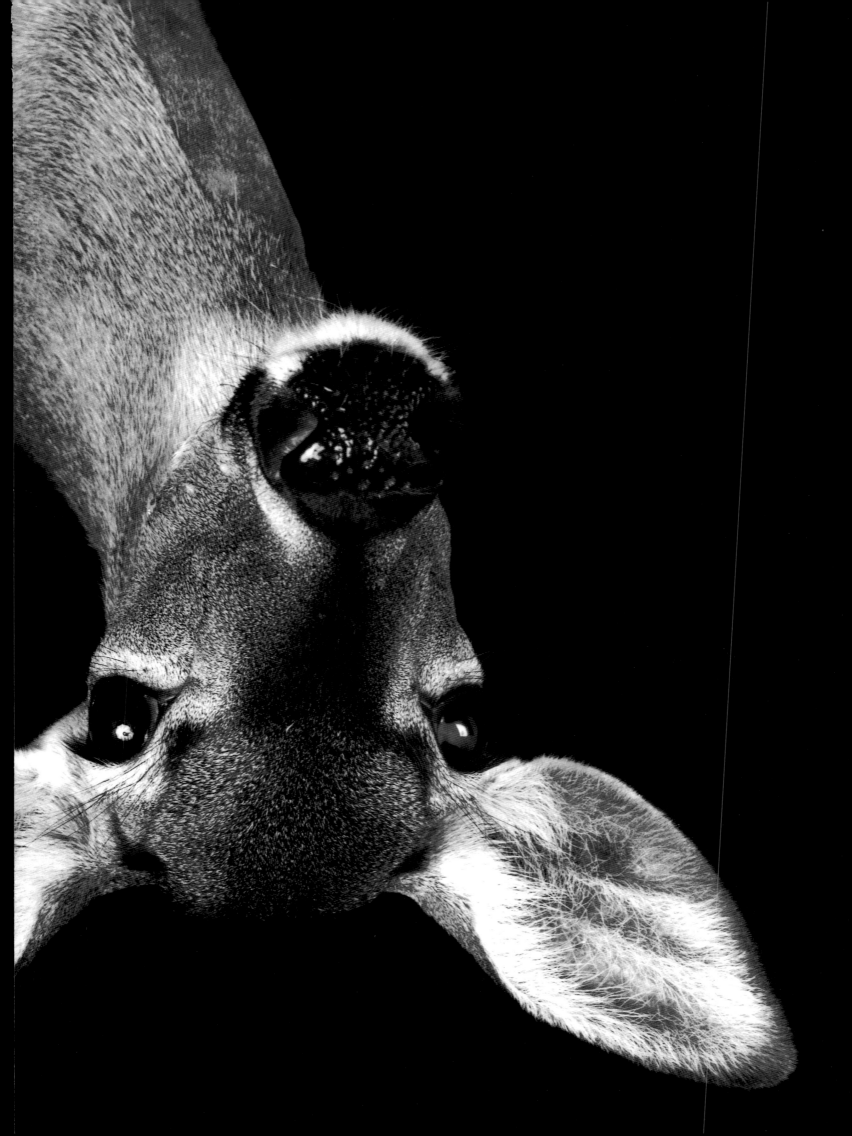

3 (preceding spread) **greg mathieson** art director: mark michaelson · director
of photography: james k. colton · publication: newsweek · publishing company: newsweek inc.
writer: douglas c. waller · unpublished image of navy seal recruits learning drown proofing
techniques for the article *hell week*, january 1994.
4-5 susan middleton and david liittschwager art director: michael carbetta · designer:
lucille tenazas · editor: caroline herter · book title: witness · publishing company:
chronicle books · authors: susan middleton and david liittschwager · series of portraits of plants
and animals listed as endangered species.

6-7 christian witkin art director: diddo ramm · photo editor: george pitts · publication: vibe · publishing company: time inc.
series for the fashion portfolio *buffalo soldiers*, october 1994.

8-9 (overleaf) **david lachapelle** art director: markus kiersztan · photography director: greg pond · publication: details · publishing company: condé nast publications, inc.
8 writer: chris moore · cable tv's comic stripper kitty g for the article *hello kitty*, november 1994. **9** foxy brown for a fashion story on brown suits, december 1994.

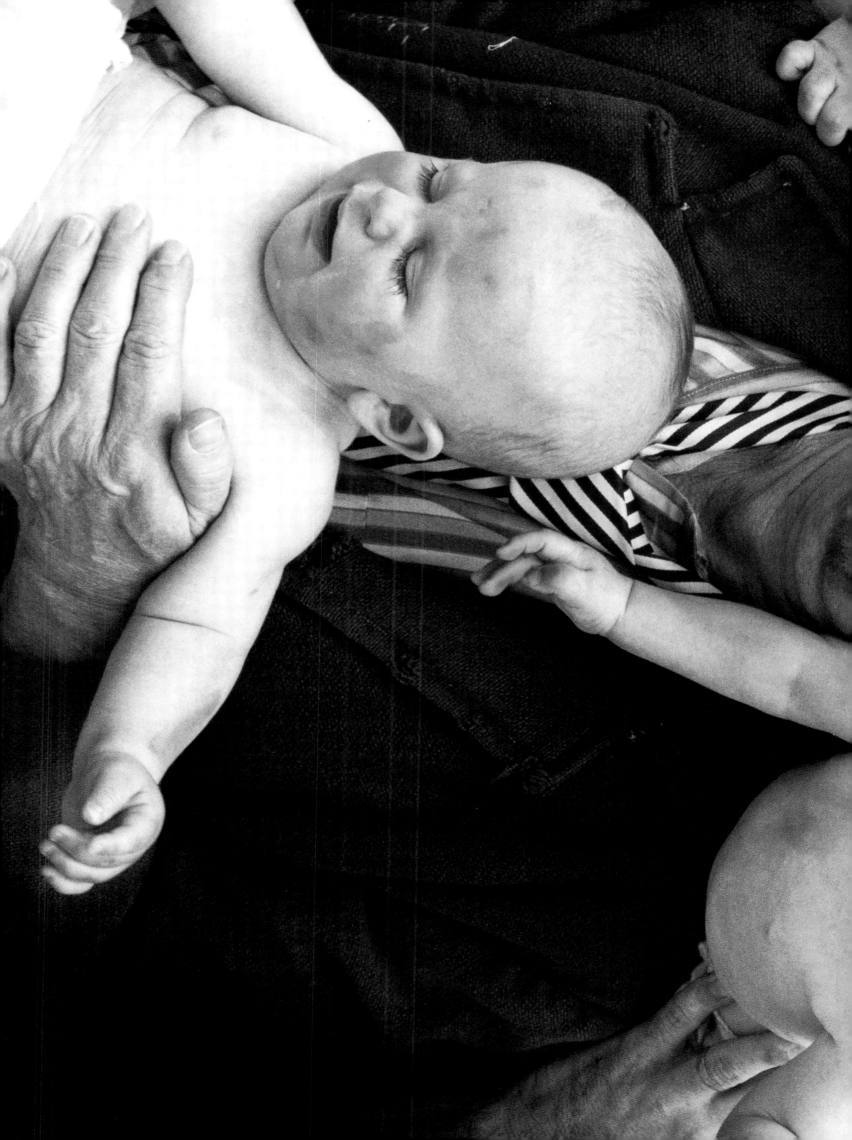

10 (preceding spread) **david lachapelle** art director: markus kiersztan · photography director: greg pond · publication: details · publishing company: condé nast publications, inc. · writer: david rensin · leslie nielsen for the interview *leslie nielsen, not exactly kenneth branagh*, april 1994.

11-13 **raymond meeks** art director: mark danzig · photo editor: deborah needleman · publication: men's journal · publishing company: wenner media, inc. commissioned, yet unpublished series from a photo essay on the south pacific island of vanuatu.

14-16 **thomas riley brummett** following series entitled re-thinking the natural.

14

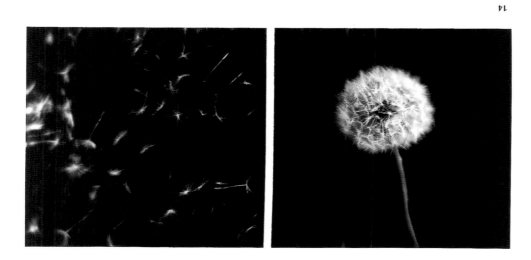

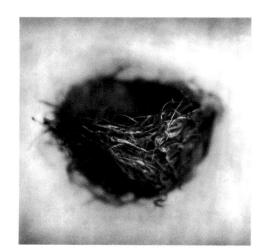

16

17 raymond meier art director: debra bishop · photo editor: jodi peckman · publication: rolling stone · publishing company: wenner media, inc. writer: toure · portrait of singer tori amos for the feature *the passion and the power*, june 30, 1994.

18-20 leon borensztein art director: janet froelich · designer: jolene cuyler · photo editor: kathy ryan
editor: jack rosenthal · publication: the new york times magazine · publishing company: the new york times company
writer: karl taro greenfield · following series from the article *speed tribes: days and nights with japan's next
generation*, june 26, 1994.

20

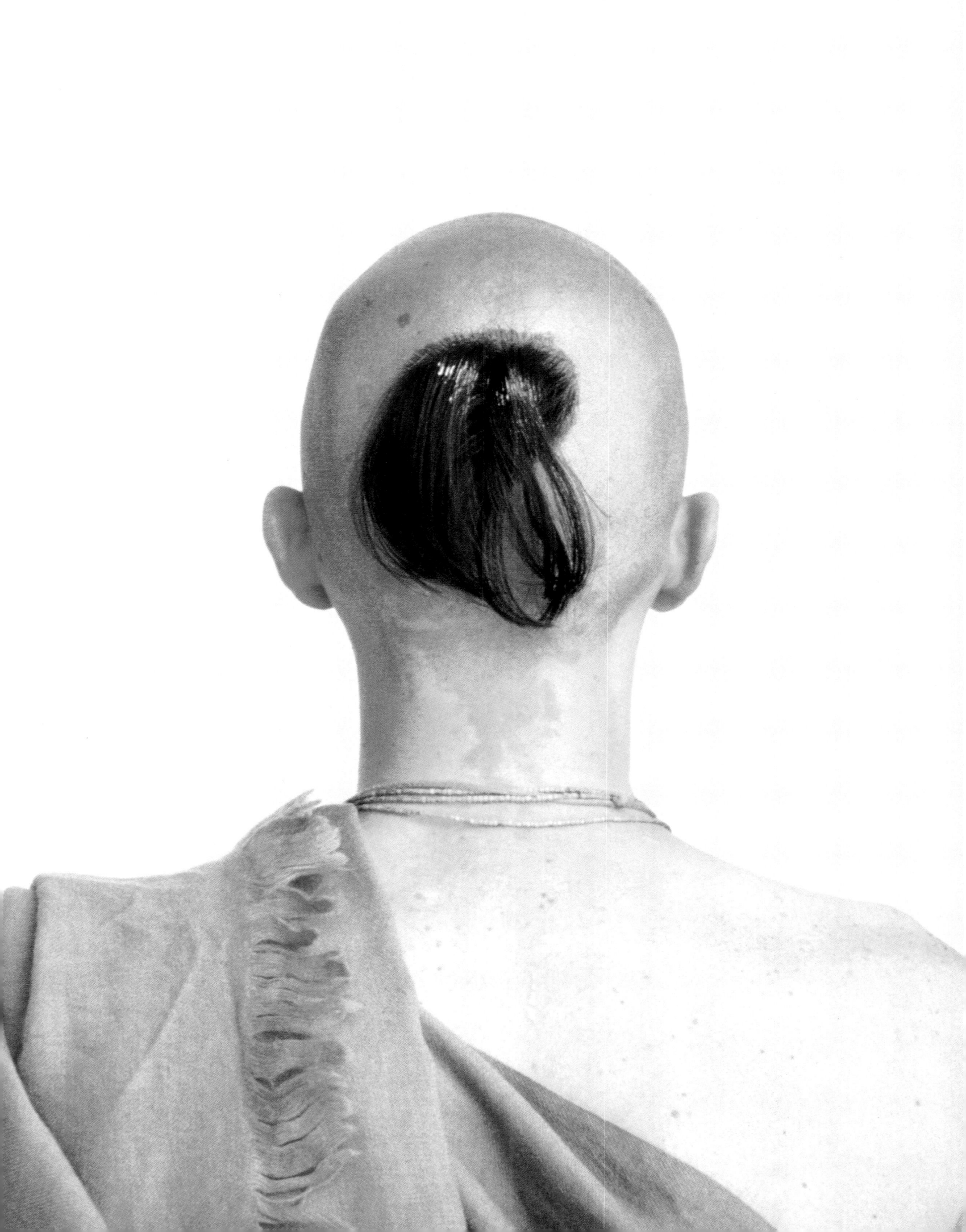

21-22 (preceding spread) **todd eberle** art director: scott stowell · photo editor: alfredo albertone · editor: alice albert · publication: colors #8 · publishing company: colors magazine · writer: alex marashian · hairstyles of the amish and hare krishna religions for the feature *hair*.
23 **slawomir zulawinski** personal piece. **24 hans silvester** art director: benoit nacci · designer: benoit nacci · book title: cats in the sun · publishing company: chronicle books · author: hans silvester · from a book on cats living on the greek islands.

25 edward gajdel creative director: sue casey · photo editor: susan b. smith · editor: mark bryant · publication: outside magazine · publishing company: mariah media, inc. writer: jane smiley · from the article *the call of the hunt*, november 1994.

26 susan middleton and david liittschwager art director: michael carbetta · designer: lucille tenazas
editor: caroline herter · book title: witness · publishing company: chronicle books · authors: susan middleton and
david liittschwager · from a book of portraits of plants and animals listed as endangered species.

27-30 russell monk art director: michael gregg · publication: the globe & mail · publishing company: thomson newspapers
commissioned series of the young victims of the rwandan disaster. **31** (overleaf) **russell monk** art director: carmen dunjko · publication: saturday night magazine
publishing company: saturday night magazine limited · writer: daniel stoffman · hutu refugees near goma, zaire for the article *open door travesty*.

32 odd r. andersen art director: jean andreuzzi · photo editor: barbara baker burrows · publication: life · publishing company: time inc.
a six month old child weighing less than four and a half pounds is shown for the feature the *color of hunger*, november 1994.
33 paula lerner design editor: j. porter · photo editor: ann card · editor: judson d. hale sr. · publication: yankee magazine · publishing company: yankee publishing inc.
writer: lynda morgenroth · preparation for the portuguese children's brotherhood festival for the article *the feasts of east cambridge*, may 1994.

34 john ficara art director: mark michaelson · director of photography: james k. colton · publication: newsweek · publishing company: newsweek inc. writers: tom morganthau, carroll borgert, john barry, gregory vistica · female cadet with classmates at westpoint academy for the article *the military fights the gender wars*, november 14, 1994. **35 david burnett** art director: jane frey · photo editor: eleanor taylor · publication: time · publishing company: time inc. · writer: hugh sidey paratroopers at the d-day 50th anniversary celebration for the article *still brave at heart*, june 20, 1994.
36-39 (overleaf) **jan staller** art director: lou dilorenzo · director of photography: bill black · associate picture editor: stephanie syrop · photo coordinator: sandy perez editor: margaret staats simmons · publication: travel holiday · publishing company: reader's digest · writer: hodding carter · series for the article *iowa state fair*, july 1994.

44

40-43 (preceding spread) **art streiber** design director: edward leida · creative director: dennis freedman · editor: patrick mccarthy · publication: w magazine · publishing company: fairchild publications · writer: glynis costin · series for the feature *show business*, a behind the scenes look at a versace production.
44 theo westenberger creative director: louis kolenda · client: smithsonian magazine · copyline: smithsonian. it's engaging · ad campaign to promote smithsonian magazine.
45 ruven afanador art director: fred woodward · deputy art director: gail anderson · assistant art directors: geraldine hessler and lee bearson · photo editors: jodi peckman and denise sfraga · publication: rolling stone · publishing company: wenner media,inc.· writer: david wild · lenny kravitz for the feature *generation next*, november 17, 1994.

46 (preceding spread) **mark seliger** art director: richard baker · photo editor: jennifer crandall · editor: james b. meigs · publication: us magazine
publishing company: wenner media, inc. · writer: jann s. wenner · commissioned, yet unpublished image of whoopi goldberg for the article *this sister's act*, april 1994.
47 dan winters art director: jill armus · photography director: mary dunn · assistant photo editor: mark jacobson · publication: entertainment weekly
publishing company: time inc. · writer: benjamin svetky · tupac shakur for the article *crying foul*, april 4, 1994.

48

48 ruven afanador art director: david armario · publication: discover magazine · publishing company: walt disney publishing
writer: edward dolnick · investigators of scientific fraud, walter stewart and ned feder for the article *science police*, february 1994.
49 ruven afanador art director: diddo ramm · photo editor: george pitts · publication: vibe · publishing company: time inc.
high cotton, for the feature *falshback*, september 1994.

50 (preceding spread) **maggie steber** · art director: mark michaelson · director of photography: james k. colton · publication: newsweek · publishing company: newsweek inc. · unpublished image of a boy shielding his face from dust as helicopters arrive with u.s. troops in haiti, october 1994.

51 (preceding spread) **larry towell** · art director: tom bentkowski · photo editor: david friend · publication: life · publishing company: time inc. · four mennonite sisters are joined by a cousin for the article endless exodus, october 1994.

52 **kevin knight** personal piece. **53 dan winters** · creative director: robert priest · designer: laura harrigan · photo editor: karen frank · editor: arthur cooper · publication: gq magazine · publishing company: condé nast publications, inc. · writers: tom junod, scott raab, peter richmond · grave marker from the article blown away, july 1994.

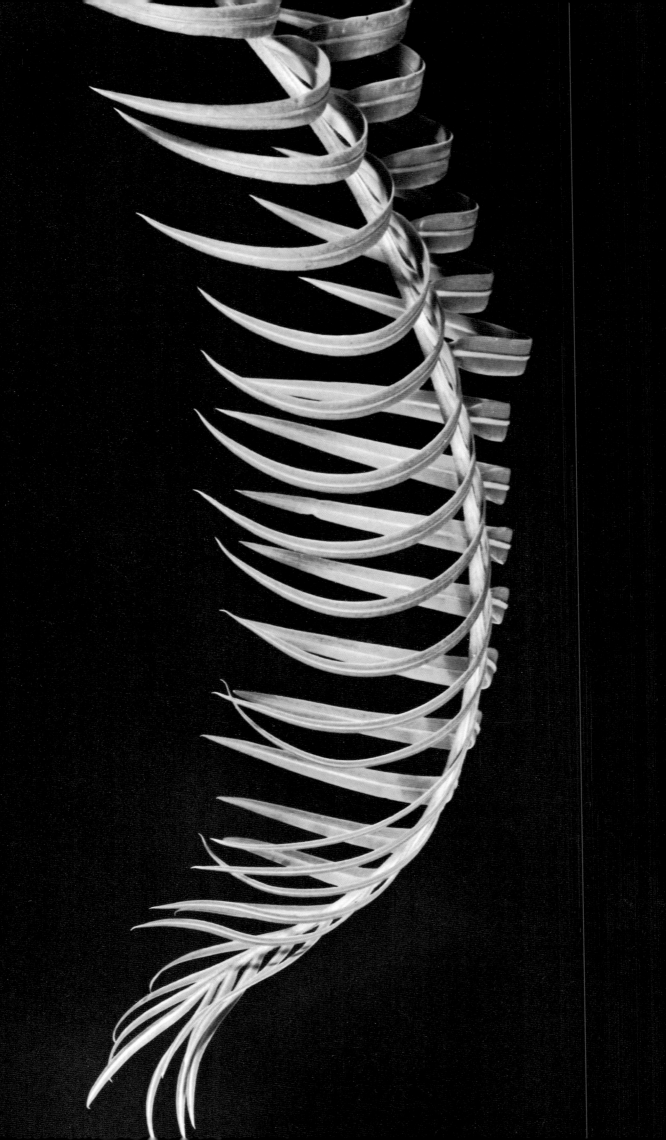

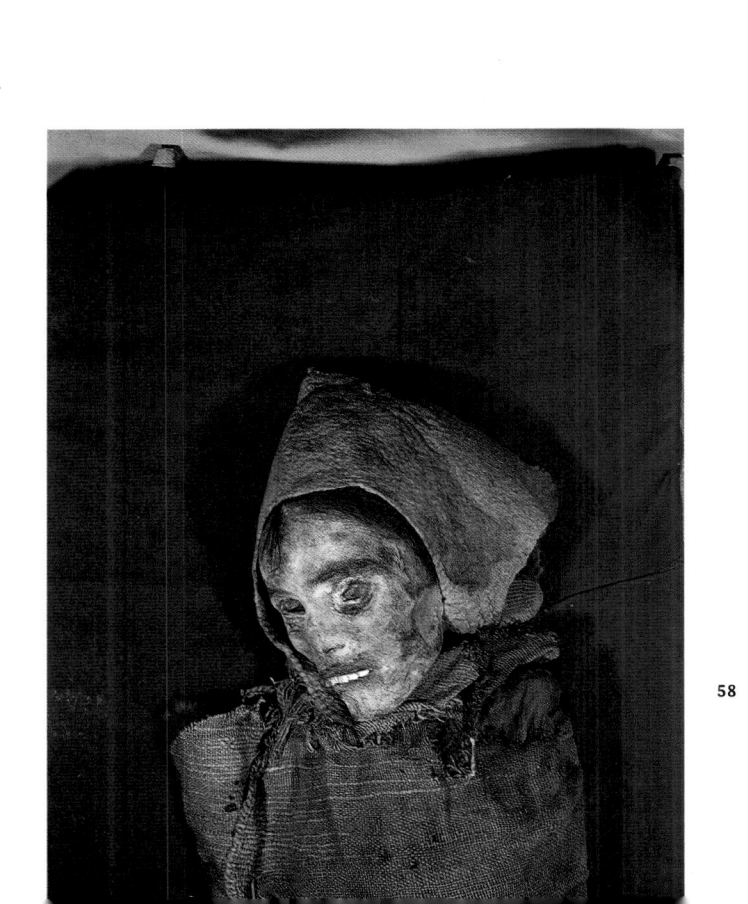

 54 (preceding spread) **thom harrell** palm frond from a series on botanical studies.
55 (preceding spread) **alex s. maclean** art director: janet froelich · photo editor: kathy ryan · editor: jack rosenthal · publication: the new york times magazine · publishing company: the new york times company · writer: james gorman · aerial view of *bone yards* where b-52 bombers are chopped-up for the article *bombers away*, june 26 1994.
56-58 jeffery newbury art director: david armario · designer: james lambertus · photo editor: john barker · publication: discover magazine · publishing company: walt disney publishing · writer: evan hadingham · series of corpses found in central asia and dating back as far a 4000 years appeared with the article, *the mummies of xinjiang*, april 1994.

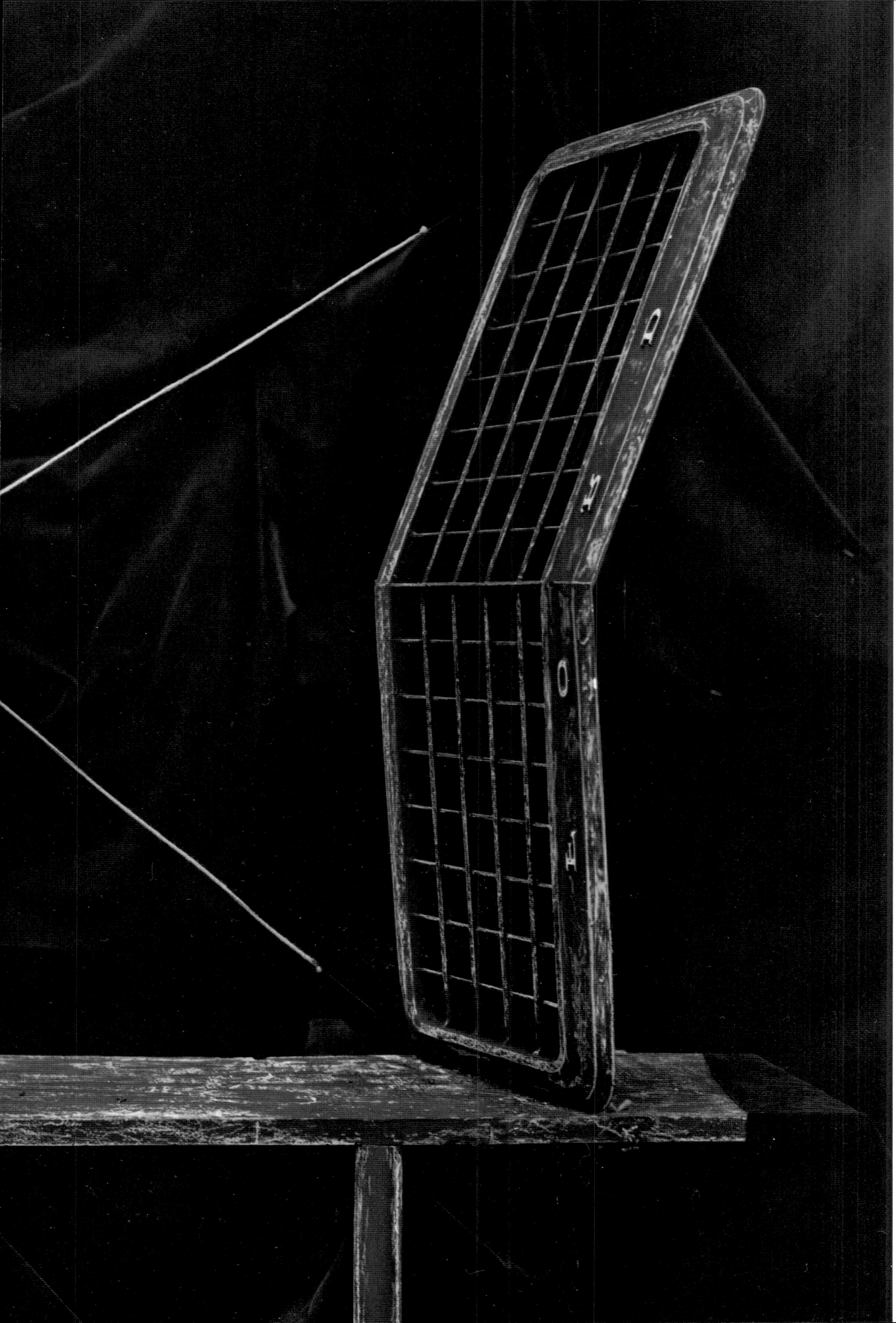
FORD

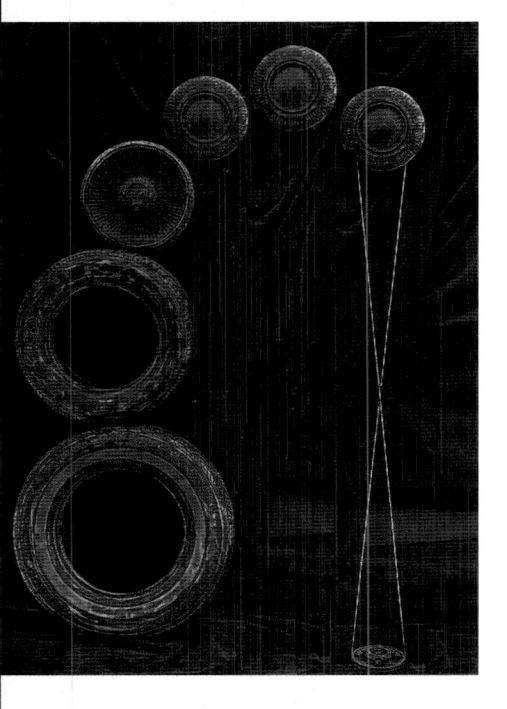

59-62 zeke berman art directors: mark schwartz and joyce nesnadny · designers: mark schwartz, joyce nesnadny and michelle moehler · copywriter: peter b. lewis
design firm: nesnadny + schwartz · client: the progressive corporation · series from the progressive corporation 1993 annual report.

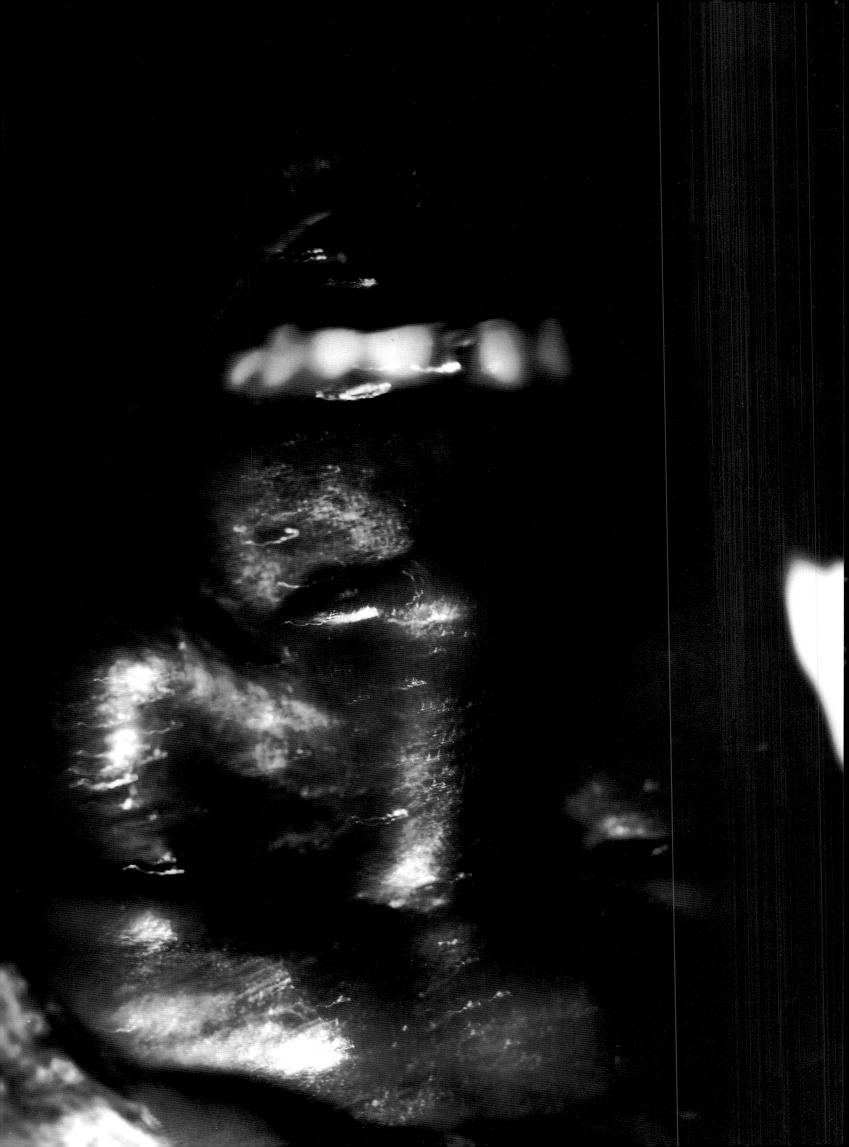

63-64 (preceding spread) **butch belair** art director: diddo ramm · photo editor: george pitts publication: vibe · publishing company: time inc. reggae artist shabba ranks for the article, *top rankin'*, october 1994.
65 jeffrey thurnher photography director: mary dunn · assistant photo editor: alice babcock · publication: entertainment weekly · publishing company: time inc. writer: dana kennedy · gaby hoffman for the feature *thirty minutes of fame*, march 25, 1994. **66 david mcglynn** personal piece entitled *wall street*.

67

67-68 jonathan exley from a series of personal pieces of chateau chambord in the loire valley, france and paris from the arch de triomphe.

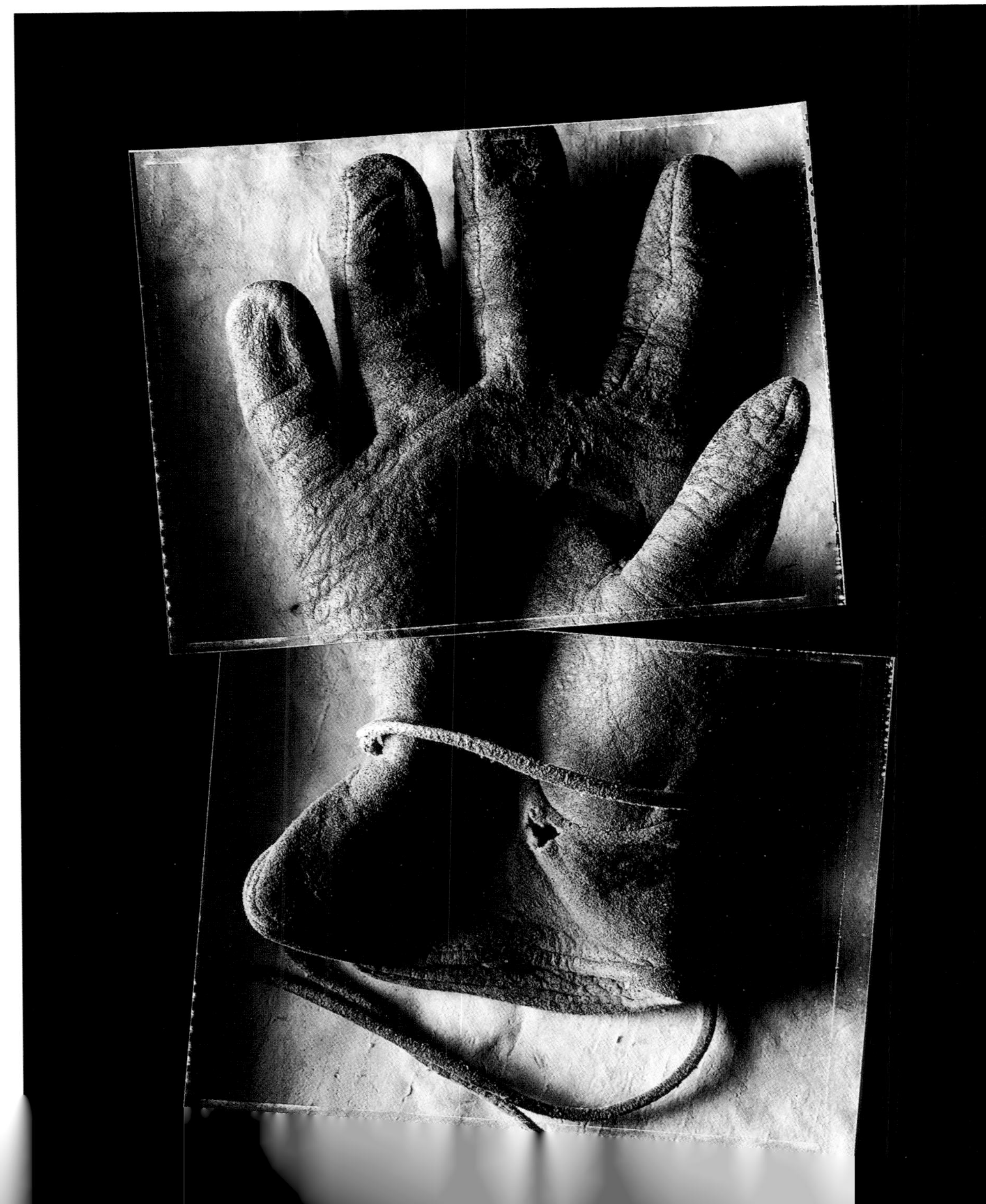

69 craig cutler from a personal
series of flowers in blue.
70-71 sean kernan guatemalan
shepherd's hat and bull rider's glove
from a series entitled *old clothes*.

72-75 (preceding spread) **karina taira** series of personal pieces. **76 maria robledo** art director: gael towey · designer: claudia bruno · photo editor: heidi posner
publication: martha stewart living · publishing company: time inc. · writer: brad kessler · cauliflower floret for the article *brassica*, november 1994.

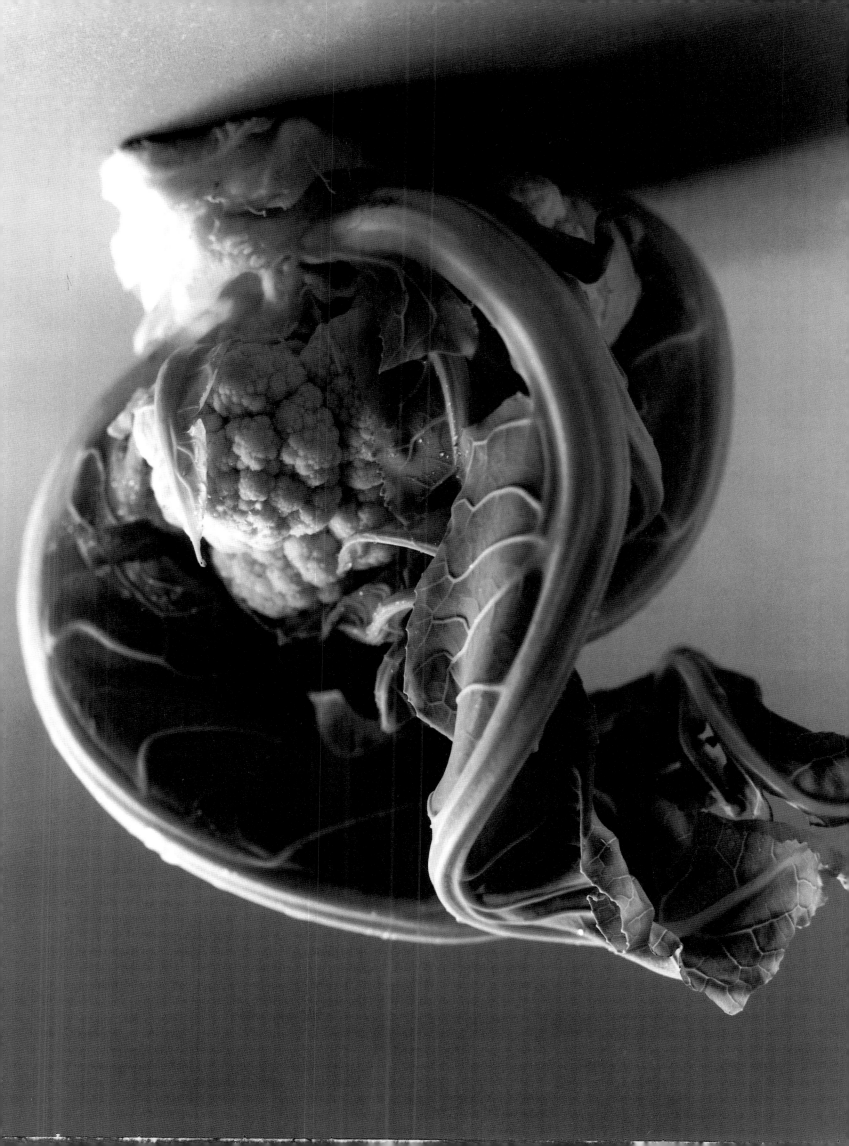

77-78 victor schrager art director: gael towey · photo editor: heidi posner · publication: martha stewart living · publishing company: time inc. · writer: brad kessler
77 the buff cochin for the article *chickens*, october 1994. **78** the partridge wyandotte bantam for the article *chickens*, october 1994.

79 raymond meeks art director: fred woodward · deputy art director: gail anderson · assistant art directors: geraldine hessler and lee bearson · photo editors: jodi peckman and denise sfraga · publication: rolling stone · publishing company: wenner media, inc. · the cranberries for the feature *generation next*, november 11, 1994.
80 stan musilek one in a series of self-promotional photographs of athletes and their respective tools.

81

81 maria robledo creative director: robert priest · designer: laura harrigan · photo editor: karen frank · editor: arthur cooper · publication: gq magazine publishing company: condé nast publications, inc. · jodhpur boot for the accessories story *30 things you can do without, september 1994.*

82 rodney smith art director: karen silveira · advertising agency: zicaardi & partners · series for ellen tracy 1994 fall fashion campaign entitled *what should i wear.*

83

83 rodney smith art director: karen silveira · advertising agency: zicaardi & partners
series for ellen tracy 1994 fall fashion campaign entitled *what should i wear*.
84 rodney smith creative director: dennis freedman · fashion editor: robert bryan
publication: w magazine men's supplement · publishing company: fairchild publications
part of a ralph lauren fashion portfolio entitled *changing stripes*, october 1994.

87

85-86 gregory heisler creative director: robert priest · designer: dina white · editor: arthur cooper · photo editor: karen frank · publication: gq magazine publishing company: condé nast publications, inc. · series for the fashion story *got-ta dance*, august 1994. **87 bev parker** personal piece entitled *key of k*.

88-89 karen kuehn art director: lou dilorenzo · director of photography: bill black · associate picture editor: stephanie syrop · photo coordinator: sandy perez · editor: margaret staats simmons · publication: travel holiday publishing company: reader's digest · writer: sam young · series for the article *lazy days*, december 1994.

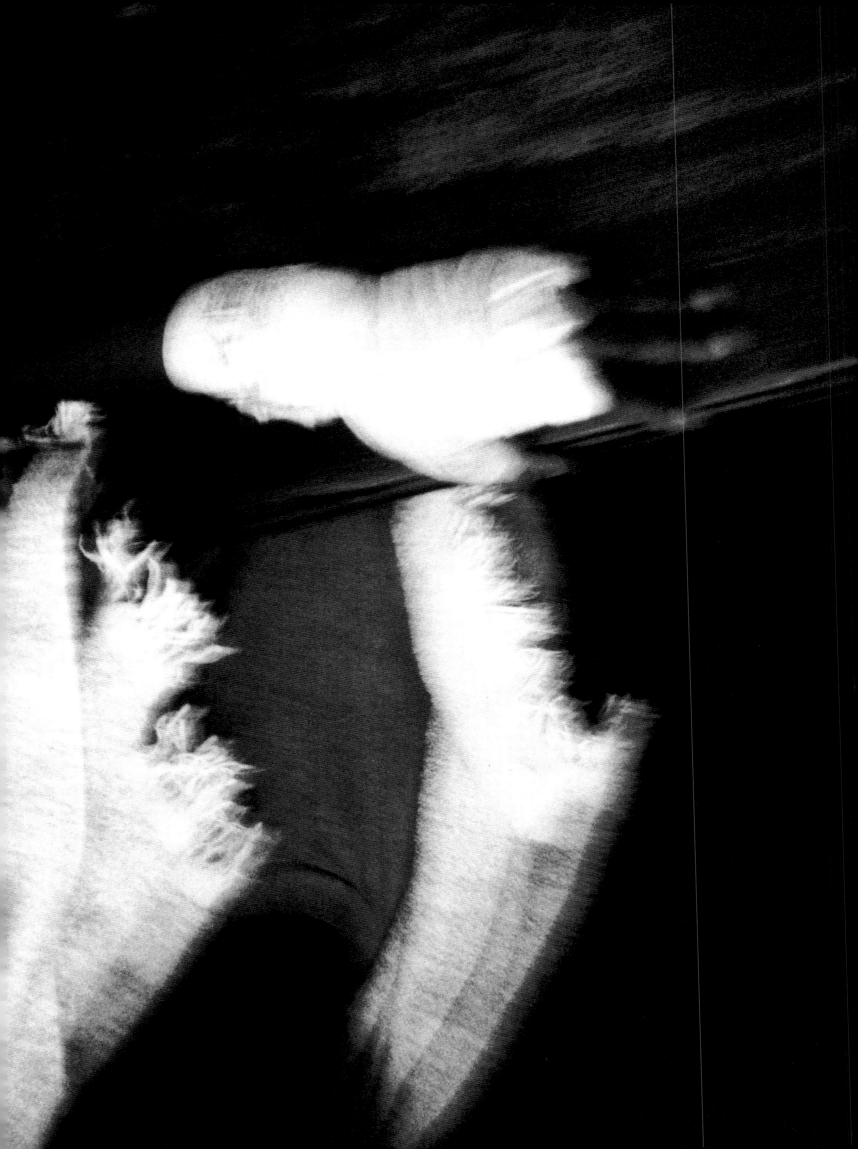

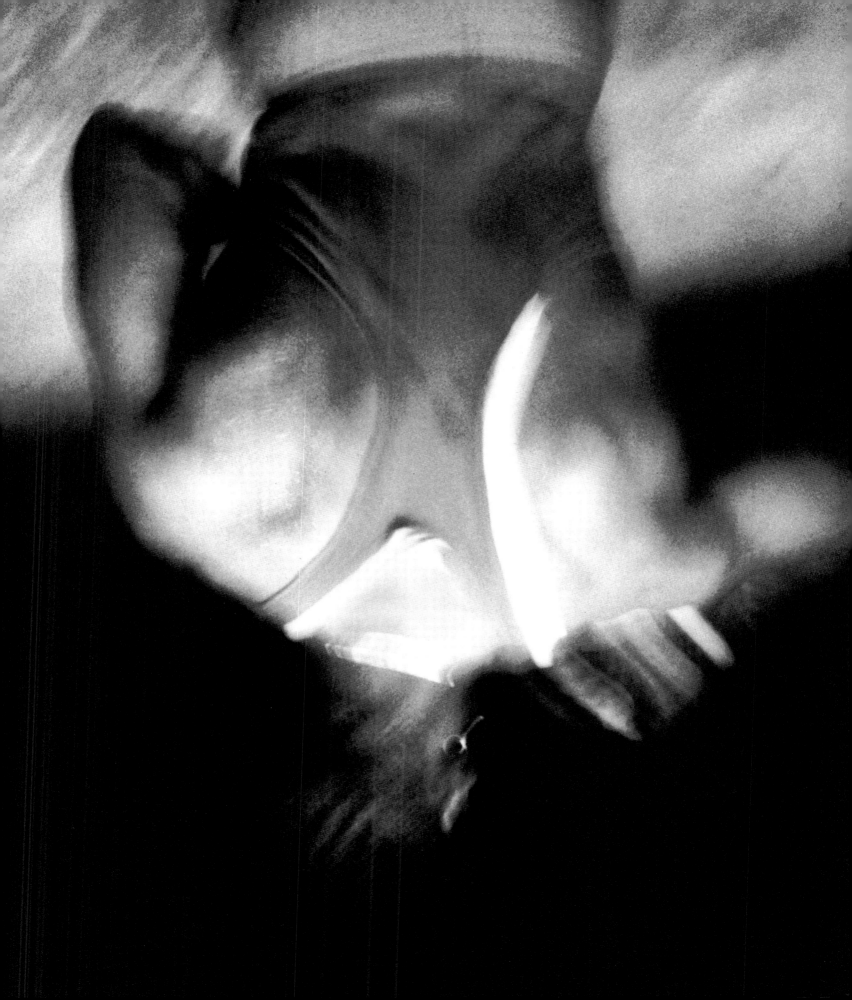

90-91 (preceding spread) **john goodman** *wrapped* and *earring* from a personal series taken at the times square gym.
92 george holz creative director: gary koepke · art director: diddo ramm · photo editor: george pitts · publication: vibe · publishing company: time inc. · writer: scott poulson-bryant · portrait of shaquille o'neal for the feature *shaq of all trades*, february 1994. **93 timothy saccenti** personal piece entitled *dj jeff*, new york city, 1995.

93

94

94 **brian smale** art director: kelly doe · photo editor: karen tanaka · publication: the washington post magazine · publishing company: the washington post company writer: bill macallister · postmaster marvin runyon for the article *can marvin runyon deliver?* 95 **mark seliger** art director: richard baker · photo editor: jennifer crandall editor: james b. meigs · publication: us magazine · publishing company: wenner media, inc. writer: mark morrison · tom hanks for the feature *the evolution of tom hanks,* august 1994. 96 (overleaf) **albert watson** design director: robert newman · photo editor: doris brautigan · publication: entertainment weekly · publishing company: time inc. writer: jeff gordonier · john travolta for the cover story *welcome back,* october 21, 1994.

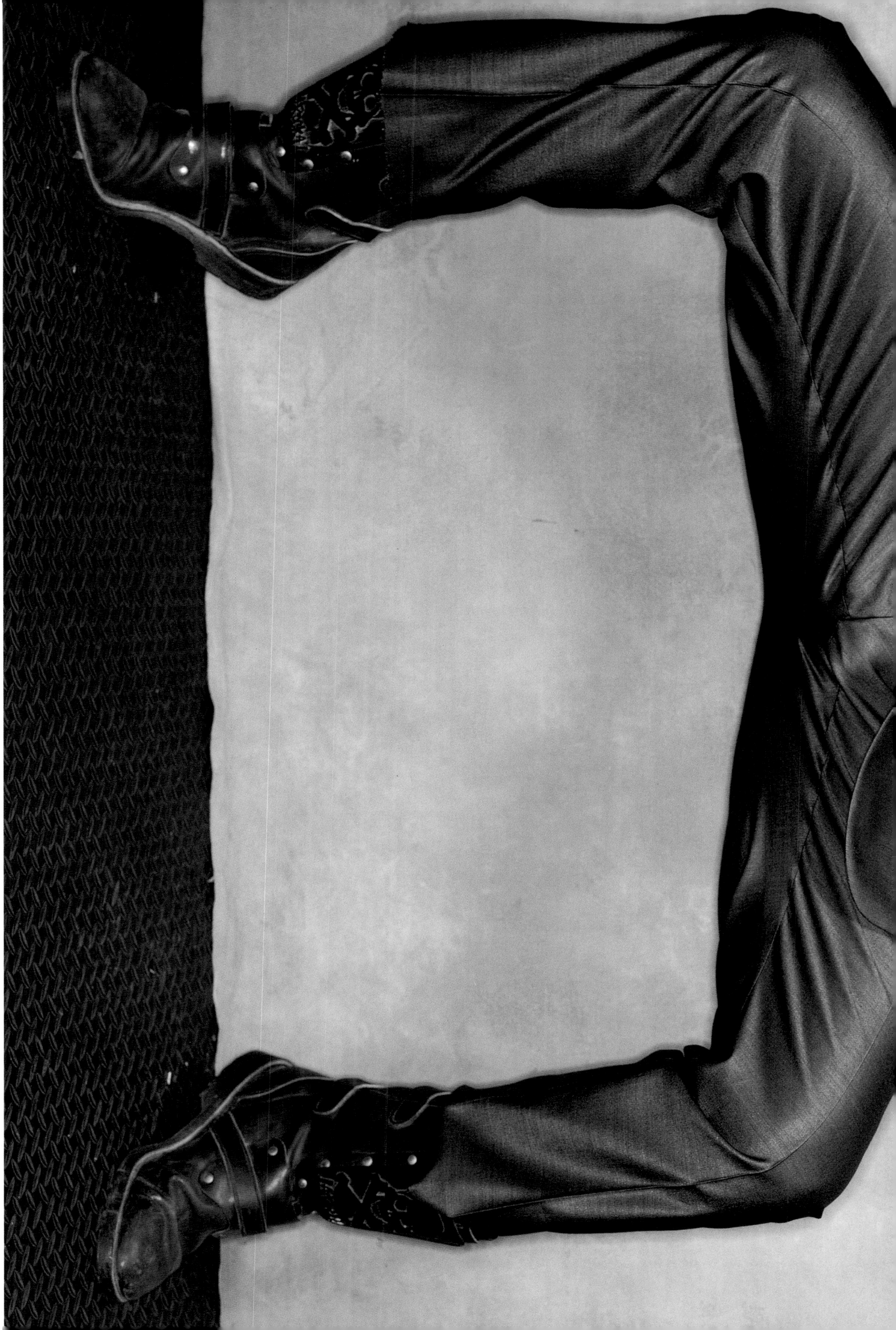

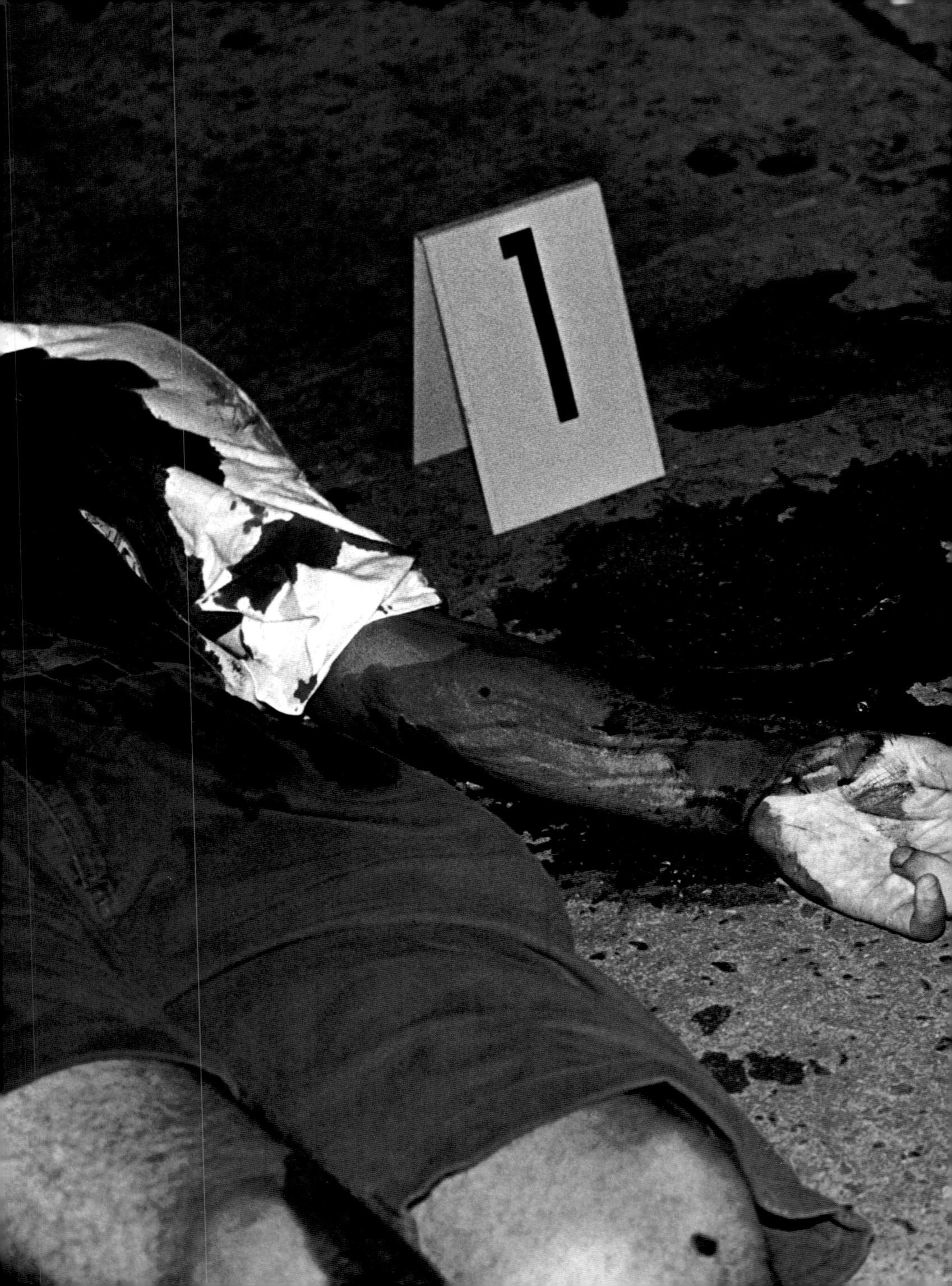

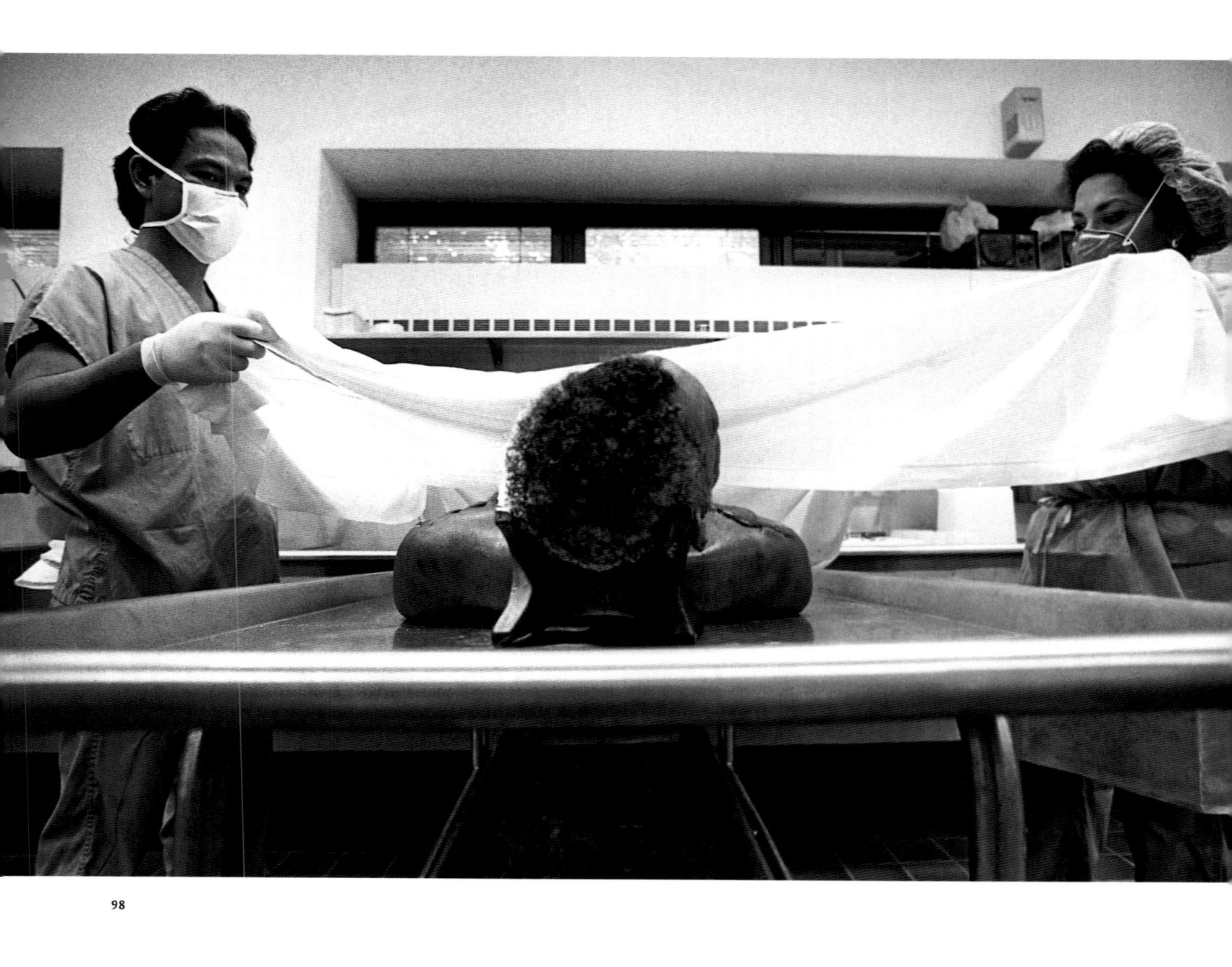

97-100 eugene richards art director: mark michaelson · director of photography: james k. colton · publication: newsweek · publishing company: newsweek inc.
writers: aric press, john mccormick, pat wingert · series for the special report *murder: a week in the death of america*, august 15, 1994.

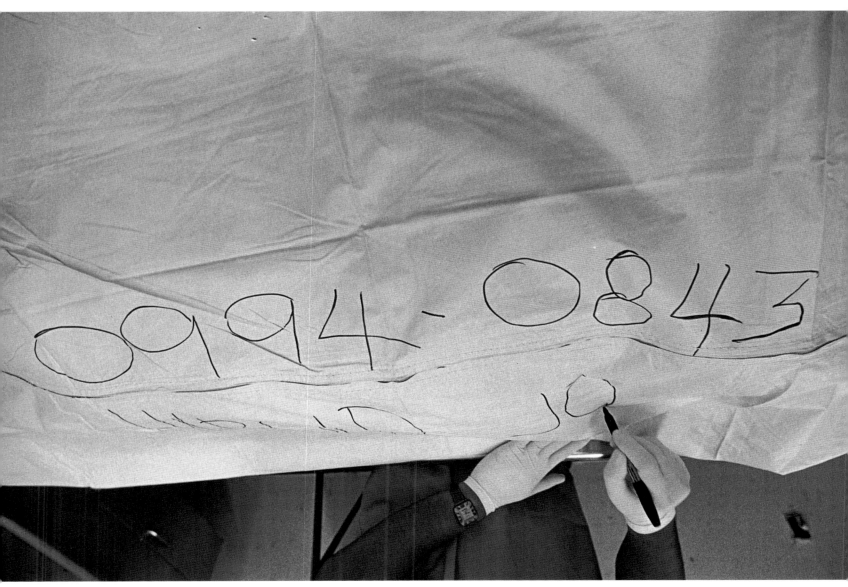

101-104 **maria robledo** self-promotional series.
105 (overleaf 2) **cheryl koralik** art director: fred woodward · deputy art director: gail anderson · assistant art directors: geraldine hessler and lee bearson · photo editors: jodi peckman and denise sfraga · publication: rolling stone · publishing company: wenner media, inc. · seal for the feature *generation next*, november 17, 1994.

106 michael schumann art director: mark michaelson · director of photography: james k. colton · publication: newsweek · publishing company: newsweek inc.
writer: eve babitz · car crushed in a california earthquake for a side-bar story *a city laid out like lace*, january 31, 1994. **107 dagny atl kimberly** personal piece.

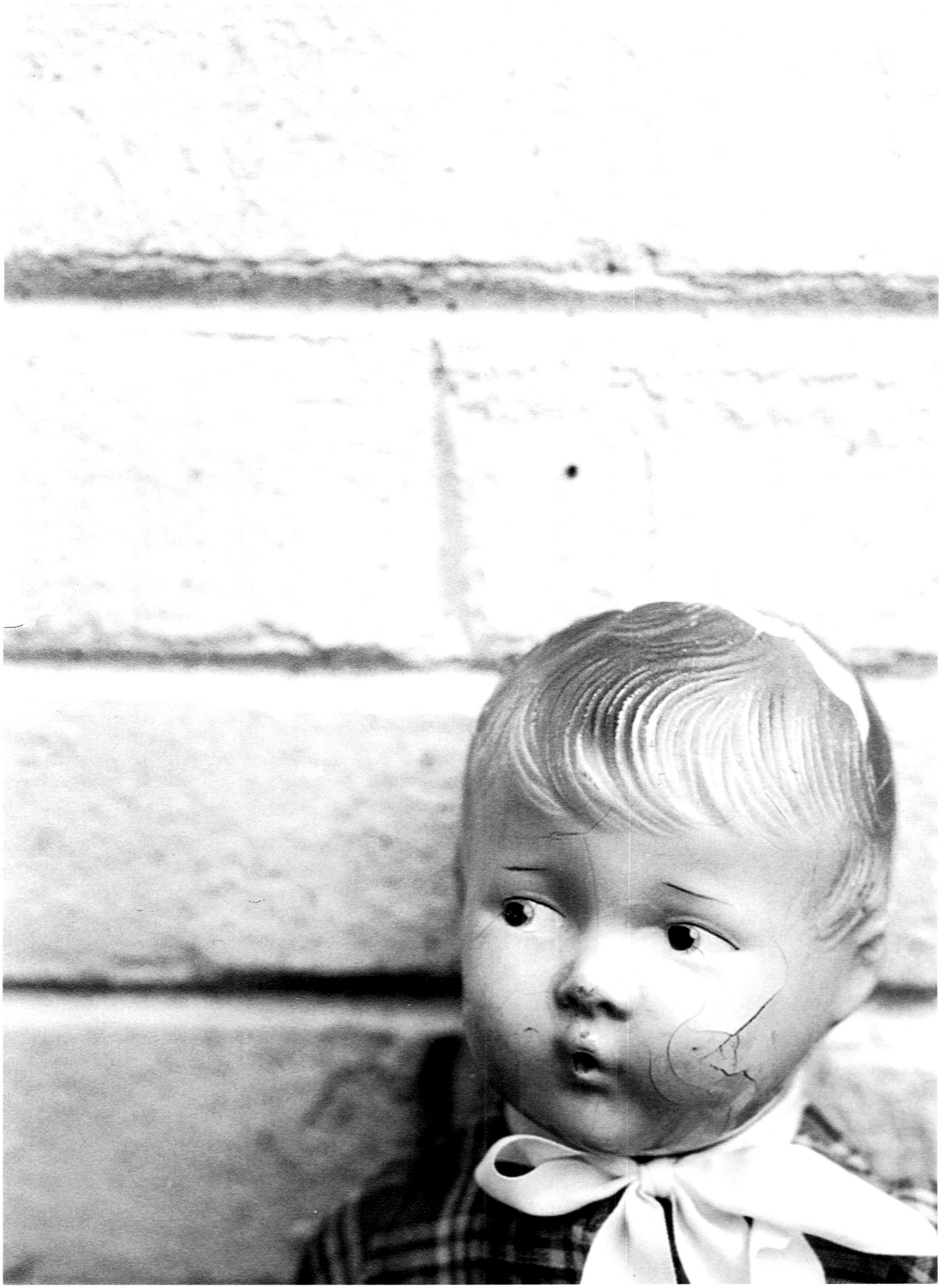

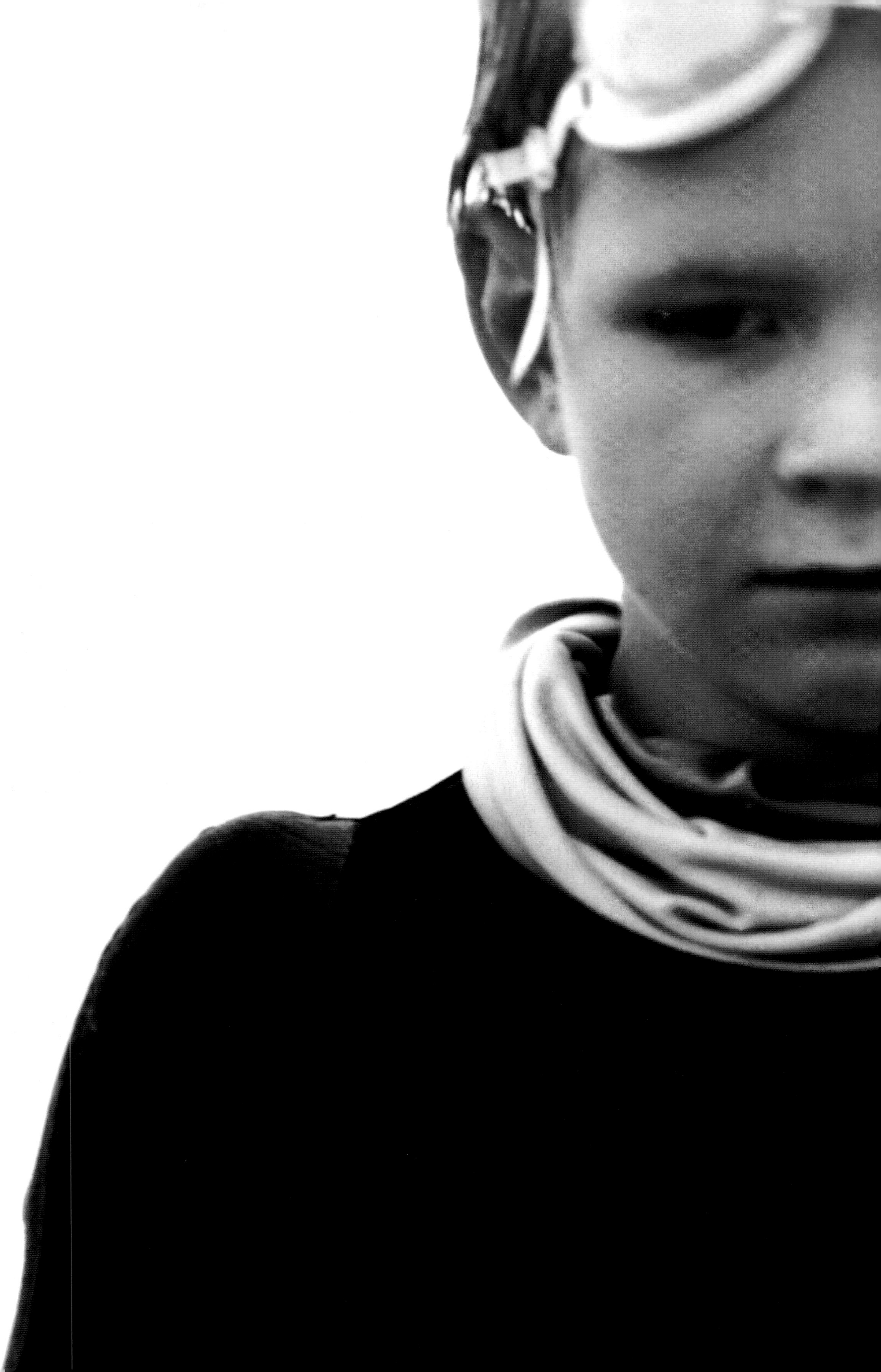

110

108-109 (preceding spread) **christine caldwell** personal series entitled *anthony ghio* and *joe ghio*.

110-111 george lange art director: jill armus · photography director: mary dunn · assistant photo editors: alice babcock and michael kochman · publication: entertainment weekly publishing company: time inc. **110** kelsey grammer for the fall tv preview issue, september 16, 1994. **111** ellen degeneres for the fall tv preview issue, september 16, 1994.

112 jeffery newbury art director: jill armus · photography director: mary dunn · assistant photo editor: mark jacobson · publication: entertainment weekly publishing company: time inc. · writer: melina gerosa · keanu reeves for the article *speed racer*, june 10, 1994.

113

113 firooz zahedi design director: michael grossman · photography director: mary dunn · photo editor: doris brautigan · publication: entertainment weekly
publishing company: time inc. · writer: dana kennedy · winona ryder for the article *women who run with the wolves*, february 11, 1994. **114 dan winters** photo editor:
doris brautigan · publication: entertainment weekly · publishing company: time inc. · writer: jess cagle · ralph finnes for the article *it's pronounced rafe fines*, march 4, 1994.

115 dan winters
unpublished image of metallica.

116-118 dan winters art director: markus kiersztan · photography director: greg pond · publication: details · publishing company: condé nast publications, inc.
writer: larry gallagher · series of zen monks for the article *soul training*, september 1994.

119 gregory heisler designer: marti golon · photo editor: david friend · publication: life · publishing company: time inc.
writer: josh simon · joni mitchell for *back to the garden*, a silver anniversary portfolio of the musicians who presided over woodstock, august 1994.
120-121 (overleaf) **m.n. kinski** series of personal pieces.

119

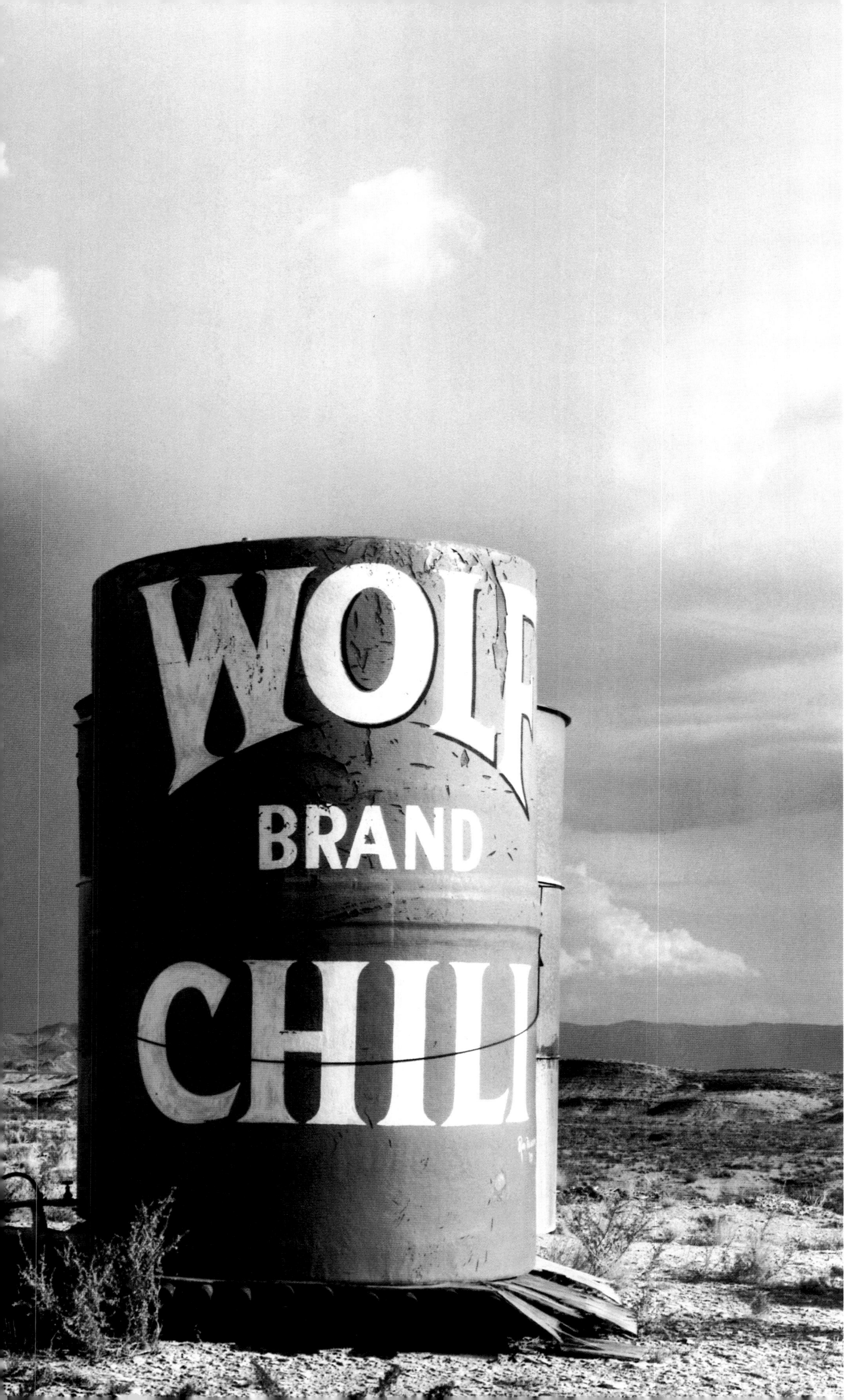
WOLF
BRAND
CHILI

122 (preceding spread) **kent barker** creative director: susan casey · photo editor: susan b. smith · publication: outside magazine · publishing company: mariah media inc. · writer: ted conover · a water tank on the u.s./mexican border for the feature *borderlands*, november 1994.

123-124 kent barker art director: kyle dreir · publication: american way magazine · publishing company: american airlines magazine publications · the jet star roller coaster and the jantzen swimmer for the article *over the boardwalk*, march 1995.

124

125

125 kent barker art director: mark danzig · photo editor: deborah needleman
publication: men's journal · publishing company: wenner media, inc. · writer: diane tegmeyer
the white oaks bar from a series for the article *on the trail of billy the kidd*, february 1995.
126 alan shortall from a series taken in the palace gardens at versailles.

127 darryl a. turner art director: james conrad · photo editor: amy steiner · editor: sarah pettit · publication: out magazine · publishing company: out publishing, inc. writer: hilton als · akuré appears for the article *i love myself when i am laughing (and then again when i am looking mean and impressive)*, october 1994.

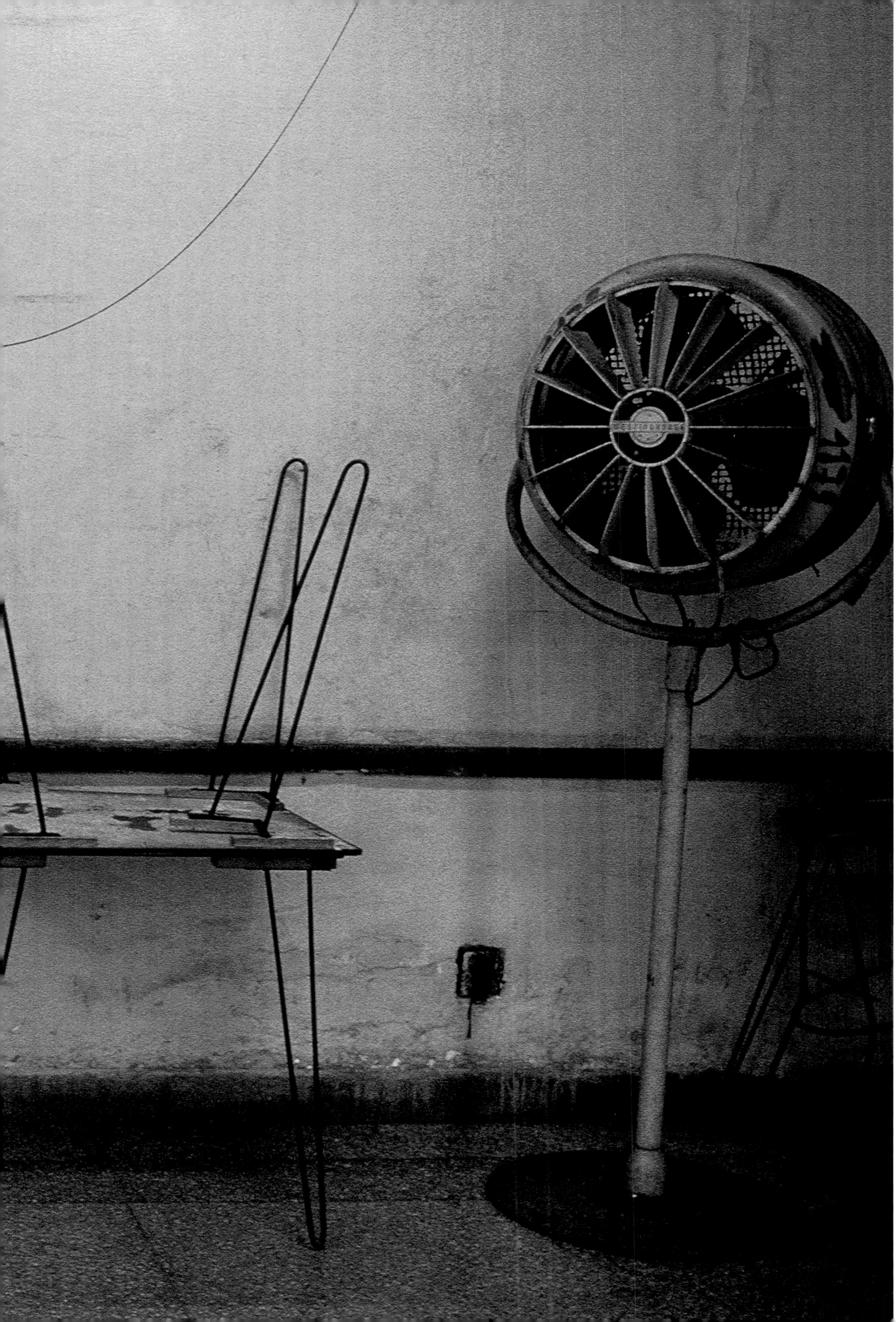

129

128 (preceding spread) **alex webb** designer: marti golon · photo editor: david friend · publication: life · publishing company: time inc. · writer: tom miller
a cuban chess club represents the depressed communist regime for the article *waiting for the end in cuba*, may 1994.
129-130 sebastião salgado art director: janet froelich · designer: petra mercker · photo editor: kathy ryan · editor: jack rosenthal · publication: the new york times magazine
publishing company: the new york times company · writer: roger rosenblatt · series for the cover story *the killer in the next tent-the surreal horror of the rwanda refugees*, june 5, 1994.

Everybody deserves a chance. Everybody.

≡ National Urban League

131 (preceding spread) **jennifer bishop**
designer: david ashton · design firm: david ashton & co. · from a self-promotional booklet.
132 mary ellen mark creative director: robert priest · designer: dina white
photo editor: karen frank · editor: arthur cooper · publication: gq magazine · publishing company:
condé nast publications · writer: tom junod · abortion doctor john bayard britton
dons what has become a necessary accessory for the article *the abortionist*, february 1995.
133-134 (overleaf) **dan winters** creative director: robert priest · designer: laura harrigan
photo editor: karen frank · editor: arthur cooper · publication: gq magazine · publishing company:
condé nast publications, inc. · writers: tom junod, scott raab, peter richmond
series for the article *blown away*, july 1994.

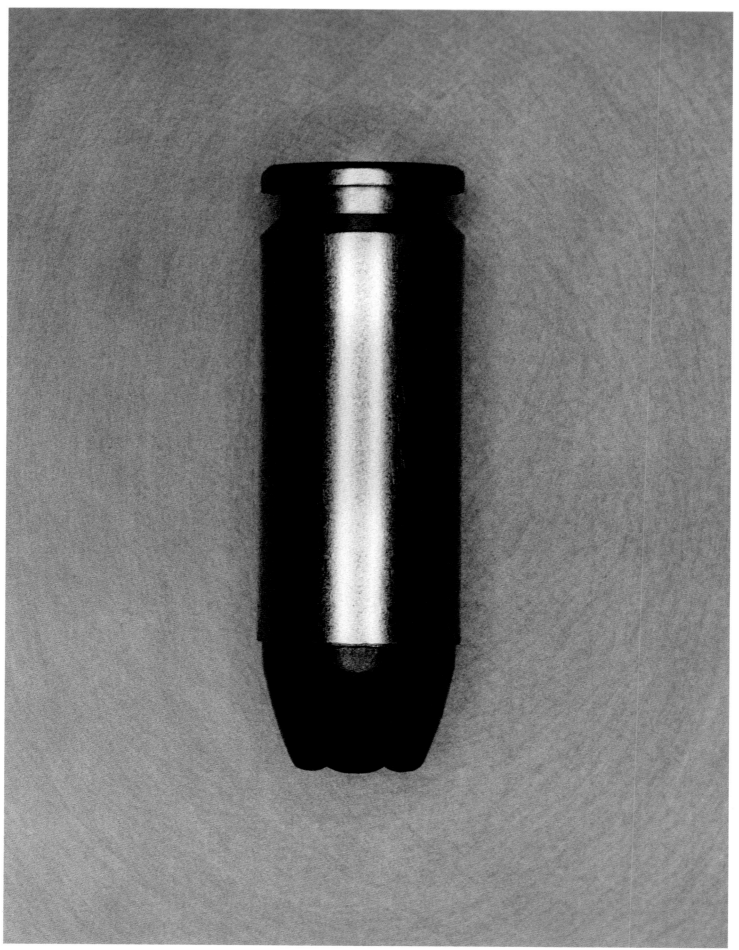

135-138 mary ellen mark art director: john korpics · photo editor: charlie holland · editor: susan lyne · publication: premiere magazine
publishing company: k-iii magazine · writer: martha southgate · series of actors from the old western movies for the article *back in the saddle again*, march 1994.

139 mark seliger art director: fred woodward · photo editor: jodi peckman · publication: rolling stone · publishing company: wenner media, inc. · writer: fred schruers jerry seinfeld for the feature *the king of prime time comedy*, september 21, 1994.

140 joseph pluchino art director: john korpics · photo editor: chris dougherty · editor: susan lyne · publication: premiere magazine publishing company: k-iii magazine · writer: sadie van gelder drag queen doodle bug at a casting call for the movie to wong foo... for the article *girl scouting*, new york special issue, 1994.

141-143 brian smale art director: carmen dunjko · editor: kenneth whyte publication: saturday night magazine · publishing company: saturday night magazine limited · writer: jacob richler · members of the cirque du soleil for the article *the cirque at work*, december 1994.

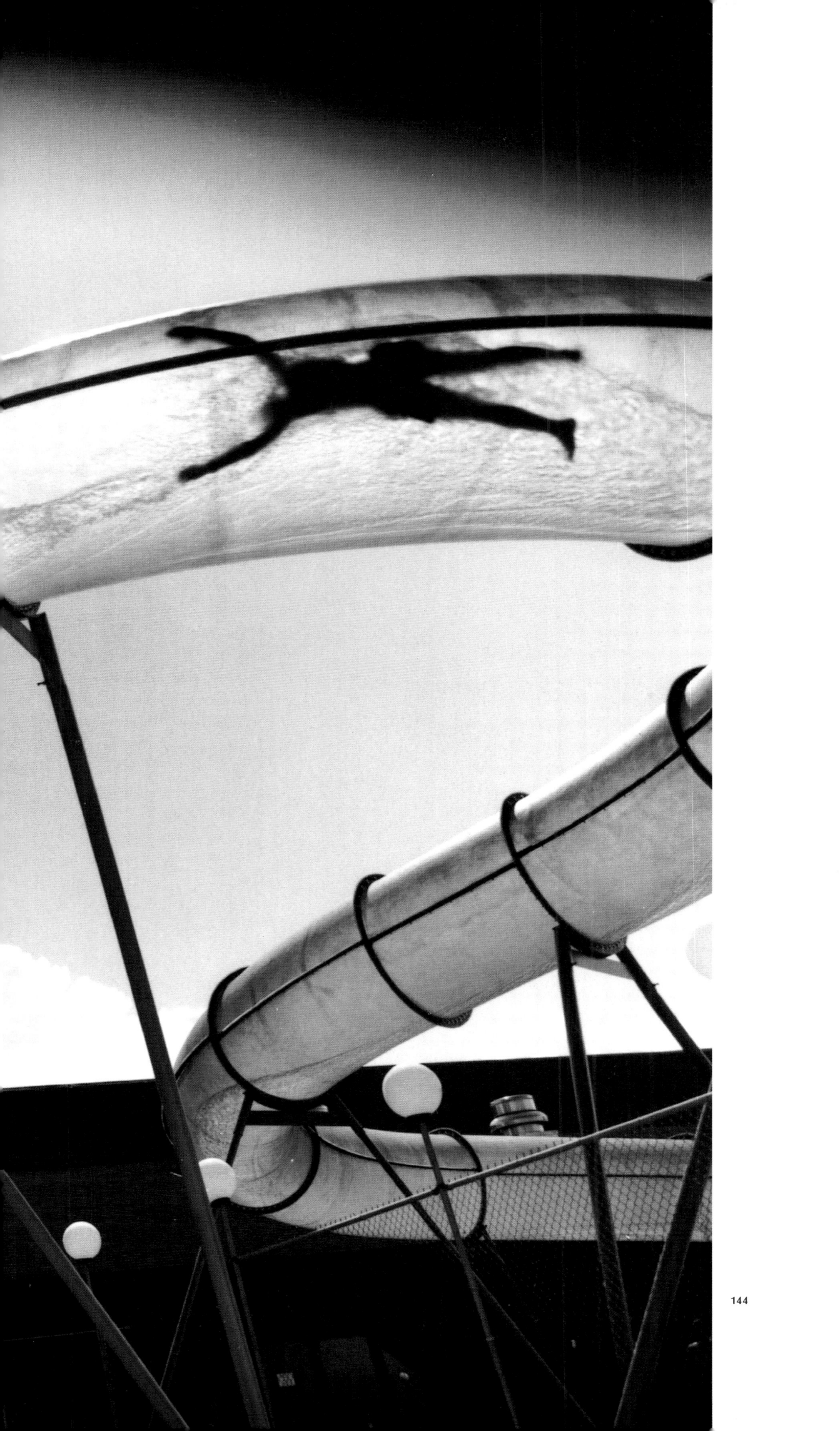

144-147 jennifer bishop   designer: david ashton · design firm: david ashton & co. · series from a self-promotional booklet.

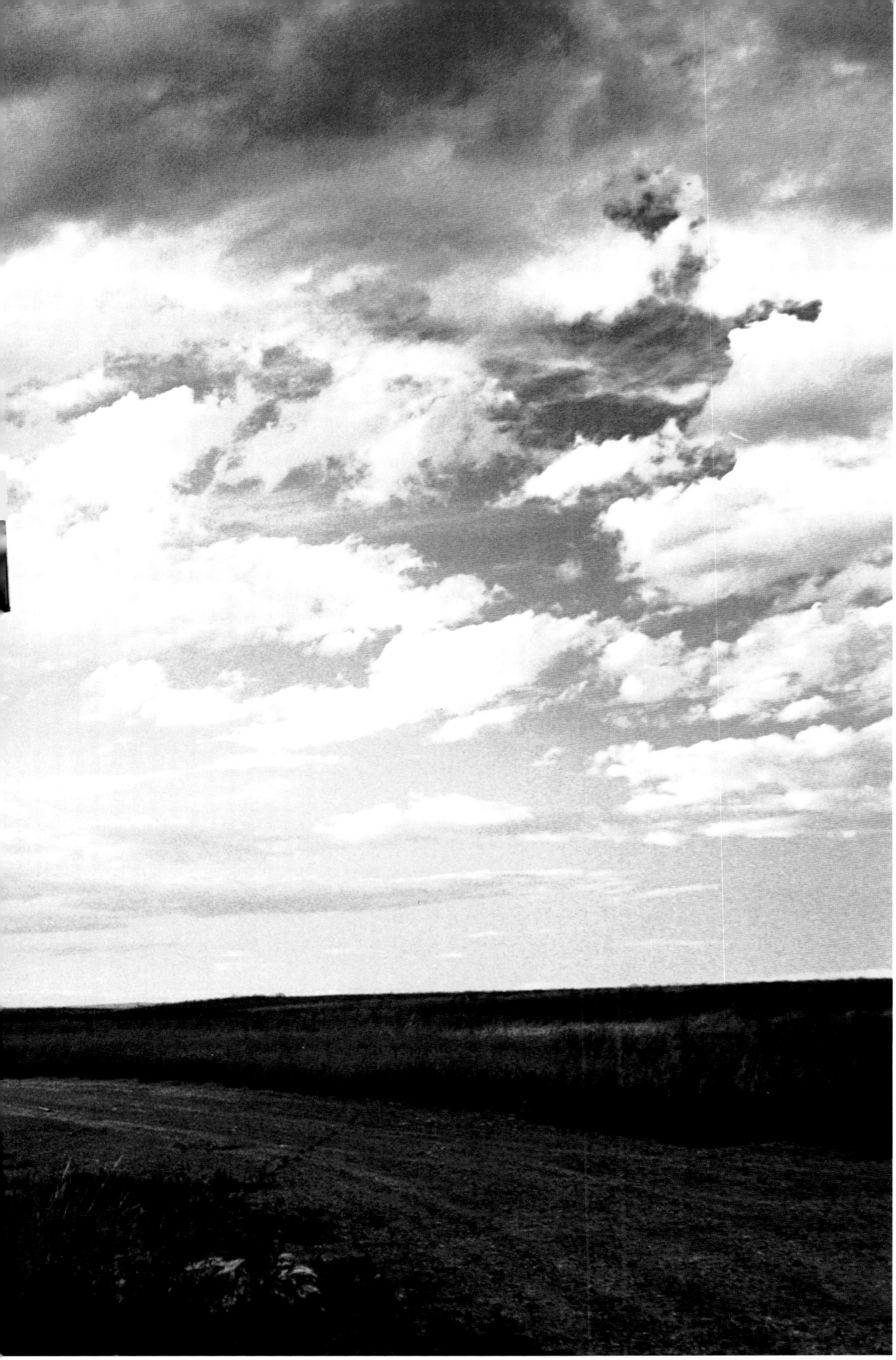

148 peggy sirota art director: john korpics · photo editor: chris dougherty · editor: susan lyne · publication: premiere magazine
publishing company: k-iii magazine · writer: lynn snowden · brad pitt for the article *brad pitt is afraid of sharks*, october 1994.

155

michele clement art director: chad farmer · creative director: paul marciano · agency: lambesis · client: guess, inc. · self-promotional piece entitled *early morning memories of childhood*, also used in an ad campaign. **155 pej behdarvand** portrait of sabisha friedberg, a personal piece.

156 beeba christopoulos personal piece entitled *rollo*, may 1994.

157-158 (preceding spread) **dan winters** creative director: gary koepke · photo editor: george pitts · publication: vibe · publishing company: time inc. writer: danyel smith · wesley snipes for the article *the trouble with wesley,* october 1993.

159 dan winters art director: kathi rota · photo editor: dawn morishige · editor: lori oliwenstein · publication: discover magazine · publishing company: walt disney publishing · writer: gary taubes · an artificial torso used to simulate laparoscopic surgery for the article *surgery in cyberspace,* december 1994.

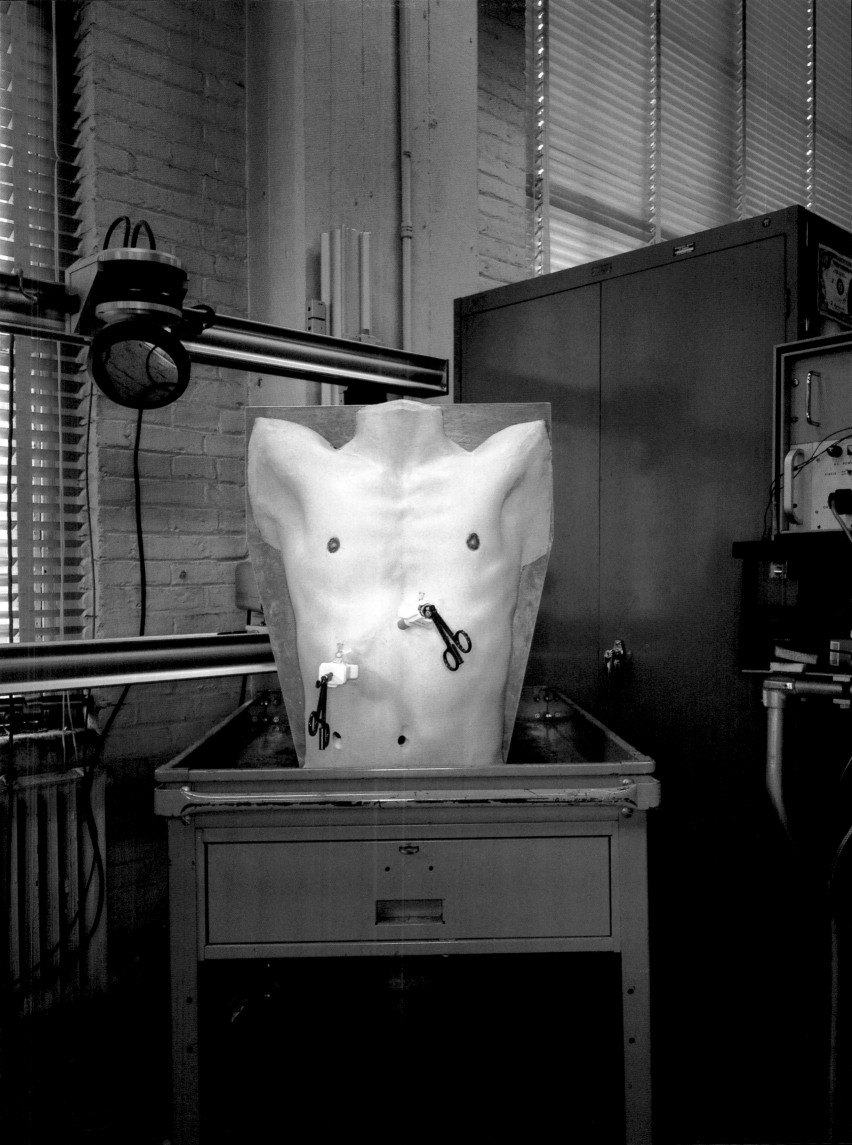

160 dan winters art director: d.j. stout · associate art director: nancy e. mcmillen
editor: gregory curtis · publication: texas monthly · publishing company: mediatex communications
writer: audrey duff · a 15-year old murder suspect awaits trial in the article *we get all hyped up.*
we do a drive-by, october 1994.

161

161 dan winters art director: jolene cuyler · designer: gigi fava · photo editor: mar!a millán · publication: working woman magazine · publishing company: lang communications · writer: elaine shannon · undercover drug enforcement officer for the article *the ice queen*, march 1994. **162 john huet** art director: mark danzig photo editor: deborah needleman · editor: john rasmus · publication: men's journal · publishing company: wenner media, inc. · writer: fred schruers skier pikabo street for the article *fearless*, december 1994-january 1995.

163 (preceding spread) **gueorgui pinkhassov** art director: janet froelich · designer: petra mercker · photo editor: kathy ryan · editor: jack rosenthal
publication: the new york times magazine · publishing company: the new york times company · writer: andrew solomon · conceptual artist beezy baily for the article *the artists of south africa: separate and equal*, march 27, 1994. **164 jon gipe** art director: mike barton · design firm: shr perceptual management · client: volkswagen golf
road trip, from the volkswagen golf 1995 dealership brochure. **165 danny turner** designer: jason barnes · publication: rough · publishing company: dallas society
of visual communications · writer: dina meek · portrait of shannon decraene for a story on former homecoming queens, october 1994.

166 josef astor art director: eva stefenson · designer: lisa daniel · design firm: calman & stefenson · publication: soho gallery series no. 1
client: steve madden · geode, parc de la villette, france, from a commemorative calendar entitled *portraits of shoes*.

LA GÉODE

167-169 mark edward harris
publication: larchmont chronicle · writer: jane gilman · sixth, seventh and eighth graders refine their social skills for the series entitled *cotillion*, april 1994.

170

170 seth resnick photo editor: suzanne richie · editor: barbara graustack · publication: the new york times · publishing company: the new york times company writer: mel gussow · artist edward gorey for the article *a little blood goes a long way*, april 21, 1994. **171 jeff baker** art director: susan noyes · self-promotional piece entitled *summer vacation*.

172 (preceding spread) **matthew septimus** personal piece shot in norway.
173 (preceding spread) **susan middleton and david liittschwager** art director:
michael carbetta · designer: lucille tenazas · editor: caroline herter · book title: witness
publishing company: chronicle books · authors: susan middleton and david liittschwager
from a book of portraits of plants and animals listed as endangered species.
174 anton corbijn art director: fred woodward · photo editor: jodi peckman
publication: rolling stone · publishing company: wenner media, inc. · writer: rich cohen
rolling stone's mick jagger for the feature *it's show time,* august 25, 1994.

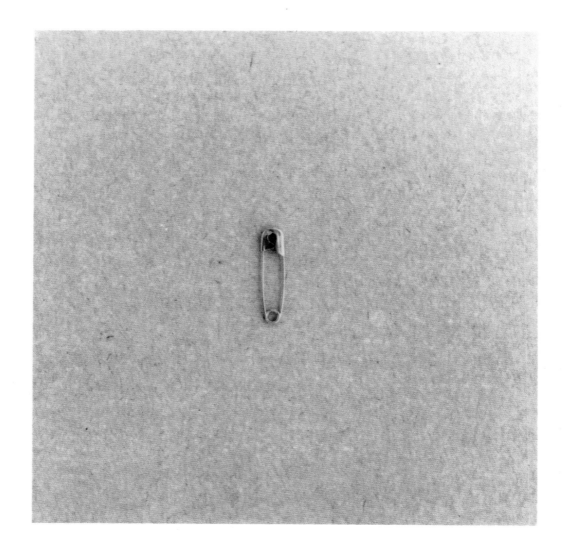

177

175 (preceding spread) **guzman** photo editors: doris brautigan and mark jacobson · publication: entertainment weekly · publishing company: time inc.
writer: jess cagle · susan sarandon for the article *laying down the law*, july 29, 1994. **176** (preceding spread) **stephanie pfriender** photo editor: doris brautigan
publication: entertainment weekly · publishing company: time inc. · writer: bruce fretts · samuel l. jackson for the article *the making of a hitman*, november 25, 1994.
177-178 christine j. sobczak two from a series of hand colored personal works.
179-180 (overleaf) **sebastião salgado** art director: fred woodward · photo editor: jodi peckman · publication: rolling stone · publishing company: wenner media, inc.
writer: joshua hammer · series from the feature *rwanda: the death of a nation*, september 22, 1995.

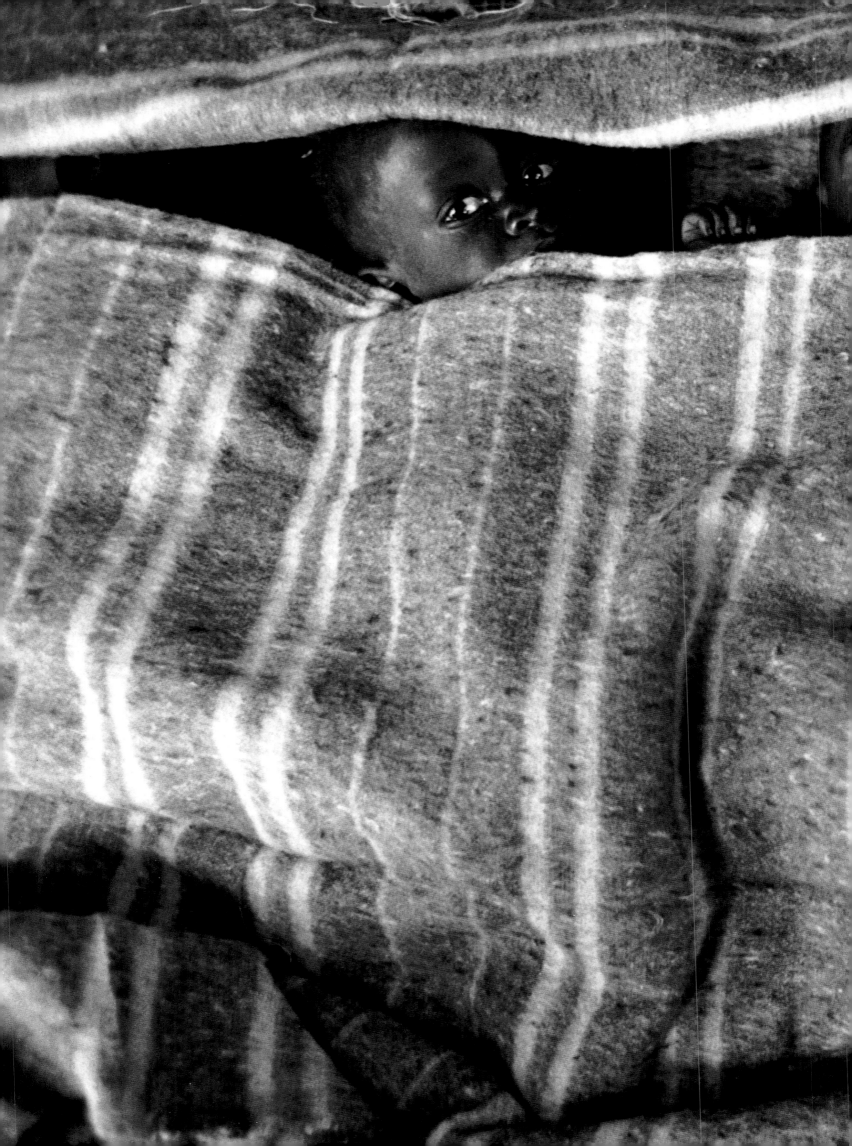

181

181 sebastião salgado art director: fred woodward · photo editor: jodi peckman · publication: rolling stone · publishing company: wenner media, inc.
writer: joseph contreras · one in a series from the photo essay mozambique: *the long road home*, december 29-january 12, 1995.
182-183 sebastião salgado art director: fred woodward · photo editor: jodi peckman · publication: rolling stone · publishing company: wenner media, inc.
writer: joshua hammer · series from the feature *rwanda: the death of a nation*, september 22, 1995.

184-185 christian witkin creative director: gary koepke · photo editor: george pitts · publication: vibe · publishing company: time inc.
buju banton for the article *no apologies, no regrets*, october 1993.
186-187 (overleaf) **carlton davis** creative director: dennis freedman · editor: rory gevis · publication: w magazine · publishing company: fairchild publications
series for the accessories feature *up to scratch*, october 1994.

188-189 (preceding spread) **dana lixenberg**
art director: diddo ramm · photo editor: george pitts
publication: vibe · publishing company: time inc. · series
for an interview on the artist formerly known as prince.
190 christian witkin art director: diddo ramm
photo editor: george pitts · publication: vibe
publishing company: time inc. · george clinton for the
feature *flashback*, september 1994.